HEART TO HEART

HEART TO HEART

▼

Bridges to Beautiful Relationships

Vicki L. Dawson & Gilbert W. Dawson

Writers Club Press
San Jose New York Lincoln Shanghai

Heart to Heart
Bridges to Beautiful Relationships

Writers Club Press
an imprint of iUniverse.com, Inc.

For information address:
iUniverse.com, Inc.
5220 S 16th, Ste. 200
Lincoln, NE 68512
www.iuniverse.com

ISBN: 0-595-18077-9

Printed in the United States of America

For all those who have loved and lost and wondered why and for those who have asked us how we have found our happily ever after.

CONTENTS

▼

FOREWORD

—————————————▼—————————————

Some women seem to lead charmed lives of incredible success in their relationships—Snow White, Cinderella—for example. Coming from a rather traumatic and dysfunctional background in their childhood, they achieve instant gratification and unending wedded bliss when they meet "Prince Charming" and then they "live happily ever after." No word from the authors(s) of those works if this is the same Prince Charming in both cases or simply another Prince in a different kingdom with the same name.

Could it be that the Prince with the foot fetish is the same Prince who wanders through the forest kissing corpses? Could Prince Charming be a philandering bigamist? And a necrophiliac to boot?

Other women, indeed—men as well—often find their "wedded bliss" is far from blissful. In fact, taking a step back in time, their intimate relationships in general, wedded or not leave a great deal to be desired. Those couples out there who get it right the first time, and they do exist—Cinderella and Snow White aside—are not the topic of conversation here. This work is for failures. It is for those people who grew up with and are still enmeshed in what has been termed a "disease of lifestyle." It is for people who need a little direction and/or polishing of their coping skills. It is for those people who's success rate is in the negative, not the positive. For people who are more successful at failing in relationships than they are at succeeding.

How can couples who truly do care for each other prevent their relationship from floundering and failing the way others before their current relationship have failed? There are many learned treatises written by very well educated people with lofty academic credentials out there. They may be very well intentioned and offer some extremely helpful thoughts and counsel, but simple, practical advice based on personal experience can far outweigh those theories. That is what is to be found here in Vicki and Gil's book. A successful sexual relationship (which is what most couples gauge success in a relationship by), neither begins nor ends with sex. It begins with trust and honesty, those themes which dominate the Dawson's book. Sex is just the icing on the cake. But.... Wow, Love that icing.

One last thought before you turn the page and begin.... No matter how true and accurate the words in this book may be, they are of no value to you unless you put them into practice. Don't just read about it...DO IT.

Nelson Herwig, LCDC

****

ACKNOWLEDGMENTS

▼

All poetry original works by Victoria Lynn Dawson from her collection *Heart Songs, A Poetic Journey Of Truth*.

Thanks to Ky for her encouragement of this project.

Thanks also to the previous relationships as this could not have been written without having had those experiences.

A very special thanks to Nelson Herwig, LCDC, whose input and review we greatly appreciate.

Thanks to Ashley for all your patience and understanding.

Thanks to Gail for your epiphany—I could not have gone on without it.

Thanks to Rachel and Daniel for believing in us.

INTRODUCTION

▼

This book was written 2500 years ago, but it had to wait till now, until pen and ink and computers, to make it possible to put into print.

Somewhere in the last two decades as women have gained their freedom, and men have become more sensitive, both have lost sight of the most valuable and meaningful part of human lives. As women have hardened their shells, and climbed the ladder of success, their ability to show real love and to enjoy not only romance, but great sex has gotten lost along the way. As men have revealed their weaker sides, and been willing to be vulnerable, their ability to love absolutely and competently, as men, and to have phenomenal sex has been buried beneath all that so called sensitivity.

This book is not for everyone. It's not for people who think their life is perfect. It's not for people who are not interested in having the most beautiful, perfect relationship possible. It's not for women who believe they are the true equal of men. It's not for men who think women are their equals.

This book is for people, men and women both, who know and understand that there are fundamental differences in the sexes. It is for people who want to know how to utilize those very differences to enhance and improve their love relationships. Yes, it is for people who want that perfect, fairy tale love *and* the best sex of their life.

Some of you are already saying bunk! But bear with us and we will share the secrets we have found, through trial and error, over a period of more than thirty years, that make it possible to have a human love which is so perfect as to touch the divine. The one promise we make to you, if you will read this entire book, is that at the end, you will have a profoundly different outlook on what love is supposed to be, how love works and how you can learn to have love as perfect as two mortal human beings can experience, and of course, the best sex you've ever had.

It is a complex picture, encompassing varied but often-interrelated topics. Truth, trust, honesty, freedom, acceptance, respect, revenge, jealousy, giving, forgiving, tolerance, hypocrisy, fear, fantasy, sex and compatibility are all part of the puzzle that, when utilized fully, will lead you and your lover to the kind of love all humans crave, but few know how to find. With all of these elements in place in your relationship, you can find your way out of the dark ages of relationships and into the bright sun of total love. But, someone must take the first step. The journey to the kind of love described in this book starts with one person—you.

We have more than thirty years experience, (more than sixty combined), searching for perfect love and perfect sex. Both of us, like most of you, have had failed relationships, at the end of which, we wondered what went wrong? Now however, at last, we have discovered what went wrong. Every part of the list mentioned above was not in place in those relationships and without every piece, the puzzle was destined never to be complete. Love was destined to fail, or at the very least, to be less than what our hearts craved, through our own faults and the faults of the person we thought we loved.

If you were going to try to overcome an addiction, let's say a drug addiction, would you go to someone that had never used drugs before? Or would you go to an addict, a reformed addict and ask him or her what it was like? How did you do it? Well, that's exactly what we are. We're not psychologists, we're not doctors, we're not people who have never had problems. We're not people who make $125,000 to $250,000 a year off the misery of other people. We're just normal, every day kind of people, who have had some incredible experiences in our lives. We are the same kind of people those of you who are reading this book are.

We're here to tell you that we didn't, and you don't, really love someone unless and until you are willing to practice every part of love. Love is a process as much as, or perhaps even more than, a state of being. Love is something you do. The kind of love you want is a choice, a decision, and a commitment. You can't go halfway and expect perfection. You can't go three-quarters of the way and find what your soul craves. Partial measures will only gain you a flat, lifeless portrait of love and mediocre, ho-hum, boring sex. But if you will commit your heart, mind and soul to learning and doing all of love, then you will find at the end, you have a true living, breathing, life enhancing, soul saving, heart mending, life perfecting work of art. You will find that not only you, but your lover as well, will be fulfilled emotionally, sexually, mentally, spiritually and physically.

Big promises? Yes. Possible? Absolutely! Should you read on? You decide.

Song Of The Soul

And there lies somewhere in between
a place that cannot be explained,
for man's nature is not clear
to those who will not listen.

For the words you hear make no sense,
unless your ears are your heart…
A name, a phrase that was your own,
can now be confused if not brought home.

And told with truth to one who will listen
to the song of your soul and
break the bonds set by man
to live the life and not the lie.

CHAPTER ONE

▼

"THE TRUTH
SHALL SET YOU FREE!"

"I could never trust anyone that much." If we've heard that phrase once, we've heard it hundreds of times over the years as we've talked with people from all walks of life. Or, "I trusted someone once and got burned. I'll never do it again." If you feel this way, then you will never, not in this lifetime, find the kind of love you're looking for. Without absolute trust in your partner and their absolute trust in you, you might as well not even be together.

Strong words? Yes. But no truer ones were ever spoken. At the heart of all relationships lies the trust issue. Trust on all levels. You have to know you can trust your mate. Your mate must know you can be trusted.

Of course there are the obvious areas that immediately spring to mind...you want to know your financial security is stable; you want to know you are physically safe; you want to know your mate isn't going to play head games with you; you want to know, without a doubt, that your mate is not going to go out behind your back and have wild, erotic sex with another partner. If your partner wants to have wild, erotic sex, then it should be with you. It's your right.

Says who? Do you honestly believe that just because you live with someone, maybe are married to that person, or plan to marry, that you are entitled to that kind of trust? Where did that entitlement come from?

The Bible, some of you may say. God said we are to cleave only to one another and forsake all others. When was the last time you read that good book from beginning to end? While God may or may not condone partners sleeping around on one another, all you have to do is read to know that examples of "infidelity" are rampant within those pages. And so are examples of men with more than one wife. There are, in fact, several hundred references to this topic. But, then technically, that's not sneaking around is it? After all, wife number one most definitely knows about wives two, three, four, etc.

What the bible does say is that the two of you shall become one flesh. Whoa! Of course, you can take that as literal and assume it means that you become one flesh when your bodies are joined sexually in the actual act of intercourse. But, we're here to tell you it means much more than that. Sure, you literally become "like" one flesh during sex, lovemaking, and intercourse. But, until your minds, your heart and your soul are truly joined, you will never be capable of a true one-flesh relationship. Don't even try.

Before you get your dander up and burn us at the stake for heresy, or at the least, toss this book in the fire, let us assure you, we aren't here to debunk anyone's religious beliefs. After all, there are far too many different religious beliefs relating to marriage, sex, and relationships to tackle in one book. Our concern is not to address each religious belief or custom. Our concern is going back prior to religion as we know it through study. Understanding man's history on this planet dates back several thousand years. Prior to organized religion man walked on this planet and had beliefs and understandings about relationships between his woman and himself and the woman understood her relationship between her and her man. In the beginning, man was in the simplest times and lived by his instincts. There were no rules, no books, to tell him this is how he should deal with relationships. He lived by his natural instinct and his abilities. Today, that genetic code is still buried within us from our distant ancestors. It matters not if you are male or female. Those codes still exist. You can unlock those closed doors and become the person you were meant to be. Unlocking these doors does not mean you will become animalistic, mean or wicked. It does mean you will find within you the totality of being male and female. You will find incredible strength in being a male. You will find the incredible power of femininity. Others will wonder at what you have found. You will become an awesome human being, because in that day man was direct and forthcoming in relationships. He did not hide from himself. This is what we will discuss in this book, not the religious outlooks or the religious values of each individual person. Those are your own private views and you may retain them.

We are simply saying you will never find the kind of true "one flesh" relationship talked about unless and until you can achieve absolute trust with your partner.

Okay, if the Bible or religion doesn't give you the right, the entitlement to complete fidelity from your partner, then what about marriage vows, you ask? Do you honestly believe that just because someone said a few words over you, and another person placed a ring on your finger, that you automatically earn the complete faithfulness of your partner?

We say no, you don't. The only way your partner will ever be completely faithful, heart, mind, soul *and body*, is when you achieve complete trust.

So what is complete trust? One thing for sure, sexual fidelity is only a very small part of the issue. The larger picture involves revealing all of who you really are to your lover, and your lover doing the same, not just the parts that are obvious.

Oh, but you say, there needs to be some mystery in a relationship to keep it fresh, to keep it alive. Mystery is fine. But if you can never solve the mystery, then eventually you'll get tired of trying and so will your partner. After all, if you're reading a good mystery novel or watching a great who done it, the point is to eventually solve the mystery. How unsatisfying if you come to the end of the book or movie and still don't have any answers, only more questions. We liken it to the old serial westerns of our youth, when the cliffhangers, as they were called, left you hanging till the next week. You had to tune in again to find the solution and know if the hero saved the day. "Same Bat time, same Bat Channel."

No one wants to do that in a relationship. That is not the way a relationship is supposed to work.

Yes, mystery is fun once in a while, but on an ongoing basis, continuing mystery will make you and your lover crazy. Cliffhangers do not work in a relationship. You must have complete honesty and trust and you want to be comfortable and know the person you are with and absolutely be able to trust that person. Mystery can be a part of your relationship, yes. That's where fantasy comes in. We'll talk about that later in this book.

If you want your relationship to grow and be alive and vibrant, then sooner or later, you'll want to know everything about your mate and your mate will want to know all about you. Every part of you. We're talking about the kind of knowing that shows up when two people who are together in heart, mind, soul and body can merely look at each other and know what the other is thinking. The kind of oneness that allows you to know exactly, without any doubt, how your mate will react in any given situation.

Perhaps the relationship between you is brand new. Of course it is impossible for you to know how or what that person will react to. However, if that person has been completely honest with you about everything they like or dislike, then you will start to build a library in your memory banks. For lack of a better term, your brain is nothing more than a memory bank, a huge library of data storage. In it you will build a reference library on this individual, day-by-day, hour-by-hour, minute-by-minute, *if you are paying attention*. It is imperative that you pay attention to everything they do. Their looks, the way they blink their eyes when you say something. Everything. With that, you will build your library and you will begin to understand how they will react and you can begin to anticipate how they will react ahead of time to any given circumstance. As you build more time with them and you put more books on your library shelves, eventually you will know them as you know your own self. They will be one with you and you will be one with them. You can do this, but you must pay attention.

Life and relationships cannot be all about yourself and your needs. If you want to build a lasting, loving, wonderful and sexually exciting and fulfilling relationship, it must be more about them than about you. You must pay more attention to them than you do even to yourself. With this, your library will be built and you will become as one. We are not talking about anyone becoming a martyr. We are talking about loving openly, honestly, fully and of giving all of yourself to the relationship. Withhold nothing.

When you achieve that kind of oneness, you have also achieved trust. And with trust comes a wholeness on your part and the part of your mate that cannot be found anywhere else.

But how do you get there? How do you achieve total oneness with another human being, especially someone who is most likely, very different from you in a lot of substantial ways? We will discuss compatibility later.

An early step is to realize that inside every human being lives several people. We're not talking about multiple personalities, however. We are talking about all the people that make you a whole person. For most of us, there still lives inside the adult, a little child, a little lost boy or girl. That child is vulnerable. That child needs nurturing, loving, ego boosting. But we've all been told to grow up, leave behind childish things. "When I was a child, I saw through a glass darkly. Now that I am grown, I see clearly." While that is true in part, it's not true completely. We can never leave the child behind. The child is part of who we are. To deny this existence is to deny part of ourselves. We need to realize that even as adults, though we may see the world more clearly than we did as children, we must hang on to that child within us if we are to accept ourselves. Because that child is the beginning creature, the formation of who we are as adults. Many of the explanations of who we are as grown up men and women lie within the mind and eye and experiences of that child.

However, until you can reveal that child, until you can trust your partner with that vulnerable little person, then you don't trust enough to have a complete relationship.

Haven't you ever wished, as an adult, that for a little while, you could run to Mom or Dad and just be comforted, held, accepted, loved? Just for being. No demands, no expectations, no resentment, no fear. Just loved for being.

Oh, boy, that's scary. Because that little kid can be ripped to shreds and no one in their right mind wants to expose themselves deliberately to a rejection of self.

But you must risk that rejection. Your little person has to have a place he or she can go and know with absolute assurance, that he or she will find acceptance. We say your chosen mate is the place to go for that acceptance. You must not be afraid to let that child out to play once in a while. And we use the word play very specifically here. Many couples often display childlike behavior early on in the relationship with such antics as spraying each other with a water hose while washing a car, or splashing each other at the beach, playing chase in the park or grabbing a quickie in a parked car. These are all very child like means of expressing ourselves. And they are totally good and necessary to a healthy relationship between adults. Particularly when it comes to sex, we need to learn to play again. But we'll get to that later.

There is, however, also the wounded child or needy child. Sometimes the stress of just being a grown up adult gets to be more than we can or want to bear and we'd like nothing better than to just shirk responsibility for a little while. There is nothing wrong with taking a day off and doing nothing. Just hanging around. No chores. No "to do" lists. Nothing. Just being together as two caring people who like each other's company. (There's that compatibility issue again).

And don't think for one moment that when your lover comes home from work, after an especially trying day, that he or she doesn't need to be pampered a bit. Just like when they were a kid and came home from school after a particularly bad day. Maybe as a kid it was getting picked last (or not at all) for the ball team. Or not making the pep squad or some club or organization or other. Or not getting invited to "the party." We were hurt. We wanted comfort. We wanted to know that we were still loved, even if we had "failed."

That needy child is still within us as adults. When we've had a bad day at work, maybe the boss blamed us for some missing report or perhaps we lost a client or didn't close a deal we'd been working on for a long time, that little child will probably rear its head and be longing for some comfort, for acceptance. It is your job to insure that child is cared for, loved and accepted, so the adult can get up again the next day and go back and do it all over again, with strength and courage and the knowledge that there is at least one person on the earth that believes in him or her.

For the person in need, it's not always easy to be honest about that need. However, if you are tuned in to your lover, you will know that need is there and you will supply it without even being asked. If you have opened your mind and heart to this other person, knowing their needs will become second nature to you. If you have and are putting the necessary work into your relationship, you will be able to discern to some extent your lover's needs.

However, no one is clairvoyant. In the early stages and in fact, always in a relationship, communication is an absolute must. Language is our primary means of communication. You have a mouth and can form words. Use it. Talk, talk, talk. Tell your lover about your needs. Ask questions of your lover and be silent. You have two ears and one mouth. You should listen twice as much as you talk. Get to know your lover intimately.

But, you may say, what about someone who fails at everything? Someone who has no drive or ambition or goals? We'll discuss that topic later as a subject of its own.

Right now, there are other "people" in the relationship we want to address.

In addition to the little child in all of us, there is also the strong, independent, I don't need anyone else person. This one is much easier to "be honest" about. After all, in our society, we are inundated with images of strong, self-sufficient people, who know what they want and know how to get there. The public persona is not so hard to share. We do it everyday. We expect it of others. And we get it, unfortunately, from our mate as well. And we give that persona free reign in our relationship with our partner. No vulnerability here. What you see is what you get.

But the strain of always being on guard, always being strong, always being right, will eventually eat away at your soul until nothing is left but a cold hard shell. Your tough, aggressive side will completely rule you and your relationship as well, if you let it. Be truthful with your mate. Believe us, your partner gets just as tired of being strong, reliable, decisive, in control as you do. Perhaps early in your relationship you each "accepted" certain roles, maybe based on individual strengths and weaknesses. That is all well and good. However, we all need to grow and expand our own personal repertoire of strengths, in particular. We all need to learn. Always having to be a certain way and accept a certain role can get not only boring but wearying as well.

Your love relationship should be a place where each can come and let down their guard, show their weaknesses. Your love relationship should be a "safe haven" from the worries and stresses and cares of the outside world. Your partner wants to shirk responsibility, once in a while. You want to be the strong one once in a while. We say go for it. Let another, more fun loving or responsible part of your personality loose.

The rogue or rebel does live within all of us. Most people learn early on to control that side of their temperaments and rightly so. Society isn't set up for a world full of rogues and rebels. But society does tolerate, even admires those few who are rebels and succeed. Society loves people who go against the grain and achieve great things.

We are not advocating chucking your whole life, turning your world upside down and moving to Tahiti. We are saying that occasionally, you need to rebel a little. You need to go against the grain, do something entirely different, out of the ordinary, even out of character. You need to be free with each other enough to express all of yourself, including the wild, wanton, sexual side.

And you need to be able to share that with your partner. You must be honest enough with your partner to say, the hell with the rules, let's break a few, if that's how you feel. If you always dress in only the most professional, business conservative manner, then try something outrageous, dress like a hooker and enjoy sharing the experience with your lover. Let your mate explore that with you. Let your mate see your rebel, your charming rogue.

From a woman's point of view, while most of us want reliability, stability, security, all the nice things of society, there is a part of us that still wants to be charmed out of our pants by that devil-may-care rogue.

And from a man's point of view, yes, men want a woman who is steady, dependable, loving, just like dear old Mom, but there isn't a man alive who hasn't at least once in his life wished for one night with a sex siren, goddess, love slave. Every man living on this planet dreams and wishes that he may find the perfect female. Even though he may not realize what he is wishing for, he just knows he wants something more complete than what he has. He may have the most perfect marriage. She is absolutely beautiful, the right height, the right education, very intelligent. Everything about her is right. But, if she doesn't have that aura of femininity about her, if she does not exude femininity, he knows he is missing something. He wants every part of female, including the slut, whore and slave, at least once in a while. But he also wants to know she is his lady, his best friend, the mother of his children. She can be all of these things.

But before you or your mate can allow these "multiple people" within you to come out safely, you must have a foundation of absolute trust and acceptance. Pure love.

So what's the point of all this talk about trust? Trust is the very foundation for the kind of love relationship this book deals with. Without absolute trust between you and your partner, in every aspect of your lives, with every part of who you are, you can never, you will never, achieve the ultimate sexual pleasure two people are capable of sharing. You will never truly love or be loved. Without trust, you will never reveal or have your mate reveal to you the other selves that live within all of us and thus fully enjoy the totality of a relationship.

A lot of you have been to or maybe even are going at present, to a Psychiatrist, a Psychologist, a Marriage Counselor, Sex Therapist, etc. In those sessions, you reveal things about yourself that you've never told another person. You talk about being scared, or your secret desires to have sex in unusual places. You tell this virtual stranger intimate details about who you really are, deep down inside. What a waste!

We don't mean to say here that the services of these professionals isn't good. By all means, they can be of tremendous assistance in helping you uncover your deepest, darkest, lightest, brightest dreams, desires, fantasies, hopes and fears about yourself. But if uncovering these things is all you do, you've only gone half way. Your portrait will never have life. Your relationship will remain as lifeless as an oil painting. No matter how beautiful on the surface, if you don't breathe the breath of trust into your relationship with your partner, you'll never find the glorious freedom of absolute love and all you will have is a pretty shell.

You trust a stranger you pay, why not trust the person you claim to love with all your heart?

Being honest about the details concerning your past makes it easier to be honest about the details regarding your future. You can build a bridge of trust by being honest. It may be something as simple as the things that you did in your past that were silly, stupid little things, like pulling a silly teenage stunt and putting nails under the tires of cars in a parking lot just to see them go flat. And that's a silly, stupid thing and maybe you are a little bit embarrassed about it as an adult, but it's a little bridge that you build towards being able to be completely honest with your mate, your partner, your lover about the things that you are now and you want to do now, including your sexual desires as well.

There is also the other side of the coin for those of us who have done some incredibly bad things, the kind of things that in your worst nightmare, you do not want any person to find out about. Guess what? If they do not know that part of you as well, you have not been completely honest and you will carry around in your own soul all the days of your life, this sneaky little dishonest side of you. You will never feel complete. You will always feel less. You will always know there is something you feel you must hide.

It is not worth it. You must tell your lover everything. Whether it's sick, or perverse, twisted, evil or mean, no matter what you've done, all of it must come out. You must tell the total, absolute, complete truth. And in the end if that person is the right one for you, these things will be accepted and understood. They will know that was a time in your life you did this, and you are embarrassed about it, you are not proud of it. They will know that your life did go on. You have cleansed your soul, not only to your partner, but in God's eyes. From that point forward, a burden will be lifted off of your shoulders and you will be able to live free as a man or as a woman. It doesn't matter if you are a female and you had sex with the entire football team in one night, or you were a prostitute on the side. Or, if you are a male and you robbed a bank, shot someone, you were a thief or you pulled off a crooked business deal that hurt a lot of people. Still, you must tell the truth. If the person you are with is the one you believe you want to spend the rest of your life with, if they are the "right" one, they will accept that truth as the truth without judgment or recriminations. You will then be free. And so will your mate. It is a mutual freeing of your souls. Telling the truth about everything else will be so much easier if you have dealt with the big issues in your past. Once you get the worst of the truth out of the way and in the open, then the little truths after that are so much easier.

You may feel it necessary to start with the smaller things. And that's fine, but you must at some point deal with the larger issues, the issues that you are ashamed of. Start by trusting them with those little things, then it will become easier to trust with larger and larger issues in your life, regardless of what they are. Begin by taking baby steps with your lover. Sit down and look each other in the eyes. You might even try this naked. Being nude when revealing secrets gives us nothing "physical" to hold onto, other than each other.

Start with something easy, some little incident from your past that is perhaps just a tiny bit embarrassing. Then move on to something bigger, something more dramatic or traumatic for you. At some point, and not necessarily on the first time out, go for the gold. Tell your lover about the one experience in your life that you absolutely to this day cannot believe you did. Ultimately, you want to be able to talk with your lover about the things that you may have gotten away with, but that today you are completely ashamed of, the things that cause you to this day, deep shame or embarrassment. When you do this, you are placing your trust in your lover. First and foremost, however, remember this is not a "pity party" or an attempt to gain sympathy. It is merely a revealing of self in what could be termed an analytical manner. You are examining events with the most trusted person you know in order to better understand yourself and your mate. It is not about judgment. It is about acceptance.

Trust, therefore, requires honesty.

THE ENEMY

▼

Evil has surrounded me all the days of my life
I have dwelled in darkness never seeing the light.

My heart is torn asunder and taken from my breast.
My sin has destroyed goodness and beauty
and left only night in my soul.

I know not how to cry out for healing power,
for my faith is gone-caught in a deceitful web of lies,
formed by the enemy's tongue, my own.

CHAPTER TWO

▼

"I Would Never Tell A Lie"

Most of you probably believe you are basically an honest person. Most of you probably are. At least on the surface. At least with the obvious things in life.

You don't, after all, lie, steal, cheat, rob, rape, pillage or any of the other things that fall outside the boundaries of societies definition of honesty. Even within your relationship, you fully believe you are being honest and truthful with your lover. After all, he or she knows what your favorite color is, what kind of movies you like to watch, your food preferences and those you despise. Your lover knows, because you've told him or her, that you prefer classical music and hate rock and roll or that nothing turns you on like country-dance music.

And your lover has told you all those things as well, in total truthfulness. Of course you are honest with one another. You wouldn't dream of lying to each other. You certainly wouldn't steal from each other. However, unless you have given absolute truth, about who you are, to your lover, then you are lying and stealing by omission. No, not outright lies, but the kind we pass off in our minds as "what they don't know can't hurt them." No matter how you try to look at it, this is still lying, through omission. That said, both people have to be willing to accept what they are told, without judgment or recriminations, because the first time either one starts using these things against the other, is when one or both will start emotional shut down and walls will be built. It's safer that way.

Lying is more than simply saying you are in one place when you are in another. Those are outright lies. For example, holding money out of your paycheck because hey, the bills are all paid and nobody is going to know the difference if you indulge yourself in some secret thing. In truth, however, that is dishonest and dishonesty is lying. In practicing any form of lying, whether direct or indirect by omission, you are robbing your partner of the most valuable thing you can give. Your total self.

Discovering the facts of a person is fairly simple. When you and your partner first got together, there were endless questions about what you liked and didn't like. And you were both basically honest about those preferences. After all, there isn't any real danger of rejection over which movies to watch, or what kind of book to read or in which restaurant to eat. It's simple to compromise on those things. This week you eat Italian, next week you eat Mexican. This week you watch an action/adventure, next week a love story. Simple. Easy. No risk.

The kind of honesty we are talking about goes way beyond the surface issues, beyond even the second layer of issues, all the way to the heart of the matter.

What is the second layer? That's where you reveal things about your past, your present, your hopes for the future. In other words, all the "acceptable" things. That's where you plan what you'll do, who you'll be, what you want out of life. You talk about your achievements in high school and college. You talk about your job successes. You rarely talk about your failures or mistakes. You talk about what kind of house you want, what kind of car to drive. You talk about how many children to have.

But it's all factual. The second layer deals with goals and dreams and hopes. Easy, concrete things, that are in themselves fairly revealing about us as people. After all, the kind of person who wants to own land in West Texas and raise horses is an entirely different kind of person from the one whose greatest dream in life is to be the best heart surgeon in the world. The young person who wants to achieve political greatness is of a far different temperament than the person whose greatest satisfaction comes from writing complex computer programs. The woman who wants six children is a much different individual than the woman who only wants one child. Or for that matter, no children.

But again, these kinds of things, these issues are still only scratching the surface of the whole person. Yes, they can tell us which personality traits are strongest in another person and perhaps reveal areas of compatibility, the importance of which we will discuss later. In the early stages of any relationship, it's easy to share your aspirations, your career goals. Your desire for a family. Those things are acceptable. Those are the kinds of things you would tell absolutely anyone, even a practical stranger.

But down deeper, beneath the persona we present to the world, the one society sees, approves of and accepts, there is much more. And some of it is scary.

Scary to the person in whom those desires and fantasies dwell. Scary for the person who shares life with them. Scary because not all of who we are is acceptable to society.

Yet, if you are ever to truly find complete satisfaction, complete fulfillment, emotionally, mentally, spiritually, and by all means, sexually, then you have to throw off some of societies expectations and be honest about all of who you are. You must be honest with your partner about your fears and your fantasies. Especially your fantasies when it comes to sexual fulfillment.

For example, Let's say you are married and the man occasionally goes out with the boys and they go to a top-less bar. Now, most men would never tell their spouses, much less take them along. Why? Because society says that nice women, good women aren't supposed to go to "those kind of places". The only women who do must surely be nothing more than tramps and whores. And certainly the women who work in those places can't be any better than prostitutes.

Wrong!

The first mistake in this scenario is that the man hid a part of who he is, denied the existence of part of himself to his lover. He lied by omission. Second, he assumed his wife had no curiosity about "those places." Now we aren't saying she would want to make a habit of frequenting top-less bars. But just once in her life, she might want to know what all the fuss is about.

So far, still fairly easy. All he has to do is admit he likes going and ask her if she would like to go. All she has to do is be willing to admit to a little curiosity, and show acceptance of this part of him. We firmly believe that men who do go to bars, topless bars in particular, without their wife's knowledge, are in fact lying to their mate. Lying by omission. And thus placing a brick in the wall that will ultimately divide them. Trust and honesty are being destroyed by "oversight." Distrust is the destroyer, fear is its weapon, overcome only by truth, trust and love.

Harder though, is that both of them have to be honest and open with each other. Not just about going and seeing, but about their real reactions. What if, to the woman's surprise, she is actually turned on by what she sees? Uh oh! Old lover boy there has no idea that the sight of another woman makes his wife want sex. And the little woman has no idea that the thought of his woman as a sex kitten, dressed, or not dressed, like the girls on stage is a real turn on for him.

So now what? Well, they could just go home and pretend that it was interesting and climb in bed as they usually do. "Thanks for the evening, it was different." Roll over and go to sleep. Or, if they're lucky, maybe one or the other will let his or her imagination take flight for a moment and they might have great sex.

At least one of them will. The one who imagines. The other is merely a recipient, not a participant. How much more satisfying if both can let go for a while, let that rebel out, let that sex goddess reign? But it takes both. If only one shares their fantasy, and the other doesn't, then you still have a lop-sided relationship. You still have only partial honesty.

You wind up with one person feeling vulnerable and exposed and worrying if and when the other one will use that "secret" information against them.

And that is the most dishonest thing of all. That is the one thing which will absolutely destroy all trust and all possibility of a completely satisfying relationship.

Over the years, on countless occasions, we have heard people doing what we've come to call "spouse-bashing." You know what we're talking about. Those little, seemingly innocent remarks that hide anger or dissatisfaction behind sweet smiles. Wives or girlfriends who talk badly about their mate to other friends, revealing their partner's weaknesses for all the world to see. You've seen it happen, and most of you have probably participated, either wittingly or unwittingly. It's easy to get carried away.

Here's the scenario: You're having lunch with a few close friends. One of them starts by complaining that Joe forgot her birthday, again. "You'd think", she says, "that after ten years, he'd remember my birthday. Sometimes I think I married an idiot." Then someone else, not to be outdone in the martyrdom competition, relates how inconsiderate her spouse, lover, partner is for leaving his dirty clothes all over the floor, even though he's been told a million times how much that act aggravates her. "I don't know why I put up with the slob," she says. "Must be because he's good in bed." General laughter.

Before you know it, everyone there is telling something about their mate they don't like, including, but certainly not limited to, his sexual prowess, but assuring all they tolerate it in the name of love.

And men do it, too. "My wife is the sweetest woman in the whole world, but she is as dumb as a box of rocks.

Couldn't keep a checkbook balanced if her life depended on it." And then laughter, isn't that cute? Or, when asked how his wife is, a man might reply, "a grouch, a bitch, and expensive." Wow! Nothing but negatives. Not one positive, kind word. We say that trouble is on the horizon.

Every time you say something bad or derogatory or negative about your partner, behind his or her back, you are breaking the bond of trust. And you are being dishonest. Even though we've heard on countless occasions this being done in a "joking" manner, we say some of the most profound truths are told in jokes. If what is coming out of your mouth about your lover is not something you would say to him or her in public, in front of the world, if it would hurt or embarrass them in even the smallest way, then don't say it to others or in front of others. Your partner should never be the "butt" of your joke or fodder for public humiliation and ridicule.

The two of you are supposed to stand up to the world together. You are supposed to be a fortress for each other where both are absolutely safe. How can your lover be absolutely honest with you about his or her weaknesses, desires, fantasies, if when his or her back is turned, they know you are going to tell all? Would you tell a person your deepest, darkest fear or reveal your secret fantasy if you thought it would become lunchroom gossip the next day? Not very likely. You have to decide what is more important, the relationship with your mate or the friendship with your coworkers or others. Silence really is golden when in a situation where others begin the bashing routine. If you can't leave, you can at least not participate.

If you want to really know your lover, then you have to be willing to be completely trustworthy with who your lover is. And if you want your lover to really know you, then you need to know as well, that he or she can be trusted with your emotional, spiritual, sexual self.

In addition to the fact that you are breaking the bond of trust, more importantly, what you are doing is destroying a piece of your own soul. Have you ever done anything in your life that you felt really bad about when looking yourself in the mirror the next day? You look in the mirror and you think, "God, I was such a jerk, just a complete moron for what I did to this person."

Well, if you bash your partner behind his or her back, or ridicule them publicly, he or she will probably never know that you bashed them in public, but you will know. You will always have that little sinking feeling in the pit of your stomach knowing you said something bad about your lover; and God forbid, what if the person you said those things to gets mad at you? Bear in mind, the people that you are sitting at the table with talking to now may be your best friend today, but best friends have the habit of becoming worst enemies, and anything you say can boomerang and come back to your partner. We have seen it happen too many times. And all that information which you supplied them while you were at the bar or over coffee, bashing your lover, guess who they are going to call, when they want to slash out and strike back at you? That's right, they're going to call your lover. Case in point, we know a couple where the man was in business with two other guys and they used to go out to bars, topless clubs. They'd talk and bash their wives and in general get into the "spouse-bashing" we were talking about. Unfortunately for this friend, the other two men decided they didn't want him as a business partner anymore. Guess who they called? They called his wife and related all the bad things he had said about her to them. At that point, not only did he have problems in his business with them trying to force him out, but all of a sudden he had marital problems out his kazoo. It was more than he could overcome and he and his wife wound up separating and finally divorcing.

The point here is, don't ever say anything that you don't want your lover to hear second hand and never make your lover the center of a derogatory remark in front of others.

Think of the dishonesty involved in the above scenario. Someone you love, someone who trusts you, shares a secret with you. The very word secret implies that no one else will know. What can be more dishonest than opening your big mouth and sharing the intimate secrets your lover has entrusted you with? Lives and careers have been wrecked by just such actions.

You have to be honest about everything, especially the little things. It's the little things that can trip you up, that can actually destroy your relationship. Bear in mind that honesty not only has a bearing on the past, but it has everything to do with the present and the future as to whether or not your mate will continue to trust in you, confide in you with all his or her little secrets, with all his or her little desires, with all his or her fantasies.

You have to be honest about every little thing. For example, let's say you got arrested for bad checks or you had a DWI when you were 21. Perhaps you shoplifted once just for the thrill and to see what it was like. Whatever it may be. Maybe your girlfriend invited you to a party, and it turned out to be a lesbian party and there were fifty girls there and you wound up having sex with 25 of them or something. What if your wife had some wild, erotic sex party with five or six guys in a hotel room at one time? What is going to happen if your lover finds out, through a mutual acquaintance, at some future date about a scenario such as those? Plenty, if you haven't revealed that information previously. As much as people may like surprises, these are not the kind of surprises most folks care about. If that fire hasn't been put out, then it's going to burn the bridge you have been building, perhaps beyond salvaging.

We know this statement goes against everything everyone has ever told you and for that matter ever told us, about revealing your past. After all, what difference does some event that occurred 20 or 25 years ago really matter at this point in your life? It matters because it is an integral part of who you are.

Both of you have to be incredibly honest about every little detail. You can't miss anything. You can't leave anything out.

We'll share a personal example here of how not telling about some event in your past that was perhaps less than honorable and that maybe you're even a little ashamed of, can impact your today.

When we first met and starting seeing each other fairly seriously, Vicki had been seeing someone else casually. The two were friends. They played racquetball together several times a week. She had been out to drinks with him. In other words, they were "friends." However, this particular young man wanted more than friendship. In fact, he wanted Vicki to be a much more intimate partner. It also turned out that this particular young man knew of Gil through another acquaintance of several years past. When the young man, we'll call him Justin (not his real name)learned of Vicki's growing relationship with Gil, he called her and related an event from Gil's past that could have been damaging. He also made up a few things to embellish the story and make it more powerful. (How's that for trust and honesty?)

It just so happened that in one of our very early conversations, we had talked about that particular event, the circumstances and the repercussions from it. As a result, when this "bearer of bad tidings" attempted to harm our relationship by "surprising" one of us with some bad information, that one was able to say, "I already know that." The possible fire had already been doused by honesty and the bridge remained strong. Had Vicki found out about this particular event in Gil's life through Justin, by surprise, she would have been much more wary of trusting Gil for not having told that himself. If he hadn't told her that, what else didn't she know about him? What other deep, dark secrets did he have in his past? The little niggle of doubt would have crept into the relationship and once it's there, it's like dropping a lit match onto tinder dry grass. It will smoke, and smolder and eventually catch to a full blaze and destroy everything you're attempting to build.

A word of caution here, however. When those little scenarios come up in your conversation with your lover, you must be prepared.

At that point, it's up to your lover to be totally accepting of what you've shared. This is no time or place for judgment or recriminations. It is the time to understand that was what you did then, that you are sorry for it, and that you are not going to do it again. It was something that happened, in your past. It is part of what made you the human being you are today. Try this as a "game" perhaps.

Start by each sharing something silly or trivial. Allow
yourself to laugh at yourself and allow your partner to
laugh with you. Then move on to something a bit more
serious, say something you may have done which hurt
someone else. Allow yourself to remember the shame and
allow your partner to comfort you and reassure you. Then
move on to a harder issue and allow yourself to be open
about your feelings and allow your partner to share those
feelings with you. In other words, don't hide. Try to put
yourself in the place of your partner and feel their emotions. Be compassionate. Have empathy. But, under no
circumstances should you allow yourself to offer recriminations or a "guilt trip" to the other. They are already car-
rying around enough guilt without you adding to that
burden by being un-accepting and un-loving.

By your sharing these past details of your life and your
partner simply accepting them without judgment or
recriminations, then you are beginning to build a bridge
of trust over which you will be able to cross the stormiest
of rivers.

Believe us, when it gets to the fantasy aspect of your
life, if you don't have a bridge of trust built, you will have
no way to cross the river that lies between the two of you,
between the fantasy and the reality of maybe fulfilling that
fantasy. Without the trust you have built over a period of
time, then you can not ever hope to realize your fantasy or
share in your lover's fantasy. Nor will your love be as intimate and whole as it was meant to be and sex will never be
as joyous, exciting and fulfilling as it was meant to be.

We have a pact between us that we never, ever talk
about each other derogatorily to another human in public.
We just don't bash. We don't get into it. We don't allow

ourselves to be dragged into spouse-bashing. If there are things that bother us, we take them at that particular time and we work them out, whatever they may be. And consequently, over the past years, we've worked out those details. We don't let things that bother us lie there, such as someone not taking out the garbage, because we have worked through the issues together and we cared enough about each other to correct those little problems. There have been bigger issues of course.

A good example of how having built a bridge of trust circumvented a problem comes from an experience early in our relationship. Because we had shared most all of the intimate details of our previous lives, including the wild romps as well as the very tame things, when an occasion presented itself where the issue of trust and belief came up, it was easy to know the truth. Correcting the little issues makes accepting and dealing with the larger ones easier.

One night while Vicki was working as a dancer (for a four month period), a girl came over to her and asked her to come over to the table where she and her husband were sitting. Gil, of course, is very flirtatious and a lot of girls would come over and sit in his lap. Vicki was very aware of this and it didn't bother her. While Vicki was at the table with the woman's husband, as requested, the wife got up and came over to Gil's table, and said "Your wife is very pissed off at you because you let all these other girls sit in your lap." He looked at her for about one second and said, "No, you're lying. Number one, she would never say that. Even if she was upset, she would never say it to you, ever." That called the girl down right there, stopped her cold in her tracks. She was looking to stir up trouble and her attempt failed. Honesty and trust keep other people from being able to drive a wedge between you.

Recently, in an emotional crisis, Vicki tried talking but she became so overly emotional that she couldn't make coherent sense. The matter was shelved until the next day, when in a more stable, not quite so emotional frame of mind, she was able to write a loving letter to Gil expressing why certain things were troubling to her. The conflict was resolved and both agreed to work on the matter further.

Also, for you men, direct and complete honesty will keep another man from being able to come between you and your woman. If he wants to cut her away from you and have her see you in a bad light, then lies and deceit on your part will very easily open the door for that to happen. Many, many relationships have been driven up on the rocks because somebody came and started spreading a bunch of lies and rumors or innuendoes for the sole purpose of causing trouble.

Our history is resplendent with examples of that type of attempt. If you are totally honest with each other, you can look at any person who may be trying to start problems and tell them, "You are full of it. My wife would never say that, never. Even if she thought it, she would never say it in public or to you." And that is the most incredible kind of trust. You can't buy it. You would kill, if need be, to preserve it. You would do anything, including being brutally honest with each other to make sure that the trust is always intact.

But how in the world can one person ever be that honest, that trusting of another human being?

ONLY LOVE

In his eyes I see adoration,
acceptance and only love,

No judgment dwells therein.

He takes me as I am
and asks for nothing more,
for I cannot give what I am not.

In his eyes I see beauty,
possibility, and only love.

No judgment dwells therein.

He wants me as I am
and wants nothing more
than what I can give, only my heart.

In his eyes I see the future,
dreams and plans, that we can share,
only with love.

No judgment dwells therein.

CHAPTER THREE

▼

"RIGHT BACK AT YOU"

The answer lies in acceptance. Your partner is who he or she is. You are not going to change them. And you can't toss out the parts you don't like and just keep those you do. Nope, your partner is a complete package. Good, bad, ugly, beautiful, baggage and all.

By the time your lover has come to you, he or she has already traveled a lot of roads. Some of those were good, some not so good. But every one of the paths your mate has journeyed down has helped shape them into the person they are. And every road you've traveled has made you who you are.

If you're honest with yourself, you may have a fairly good grip on who you are. You may have by this time, admitted your failings, acknowledged your successes, even tried out a fantasy or two. If not, then now is the time for some serious soul searching. Need a little help? Trust your mate and ask. You may be surprised at the revelations one close to you can give you. And, if you'll listen, you'll learn a lot about your mate in the process as well.

But what does acceptance mean? Webster's defines it as the act of taking or receiving something offered; favorable reception, approval; favor; the act of assenting or believing; the fact or state of being accepted or acceptable.

We can take that one step further and look at the word acceptable. You are acceptable when you are capable or worthy of being accepted; pleasing to the receiver; agreeable; welcome. To accept means to receive with approval or favor, to receive without adverse (negative) reaction.

With a list like that, it's no wonder accepting our mate is so difficult. After all, if you are a neat freak and your partner is a slob, that's pretty hard to deal with day after day. But, our guess is, you knew that weakness when you first got together with your lover.

The mistake you probably made was in thinking you could change him or her. Big mistake. You can not change another person. No way, no how. You can learn to tolerate those things that "make you crazy", but we'll deal with that issue later. For now, let's look closely at acceptance.

There is no greater gift you can give to the person you love than to receive them with favor. Your approval may be the single biggest factor in your lover's life. Just knowing that another person accepts us for who we are, and loves us anyway, is a powerful aphrodisiac. Knowing, whether we succeed or fail, that our mate will still love, approve, admire, respect and believe in us, is a remarkably freeing thing.

How many of you have watched your lover attempt something, be it small or great, and seen them fail? What did you do? Did you berate your partner, tell him or her how stupid he or she was for trying such a stupid thing? Did you make fun of them in front of others? Did you fume silently? Did you withhold favors? (A female's favorite trick) What did you get? Well, our guess is that your partner didn't ever take any risk again, not in business and certainly not with you. Your lover, after the brow beating resulting from the first failure, isn't going to do anything to upset the apple cart and have to endure either a tongue lashing, public ridicule or cold shoulders again.

In addition to the fact that you have destroyed your partner's ability to take risks, make decisions, even gamble with the future of your lives, you have also cheated yourself without even realizing you have done so. You have hurt yourself in such a way that you won't get over it. You will have placed a brick in the wall and begun to construct a barrier to a whole relationship. The damage is not just one-sided. It goes both ways. How will you handle his failure or her failure or his success or her success?

In reality, it is easy to handle success. It is the failures and how we handle them that will determine what your relationship will become in the future. Will it be destroyed or will it be raised to a new, higher level, with even more trust? How you handle this will make a big difference in your lives.

We also know, that because you rejected his or her failure, you in a sense rejected him or her on a much deeper level. So then your partner went out and did the right thing, and now you have all the security you could possibly want. But guess what? You're miserable and so is your mate.

Why? Because the message came through loud and clear. You are only acceptable if you are successful. Trying isn't good enough. Taking risk is not allowed. You have to do the right thing, you have to succeed. Otherwise, you aren't good enough as a person. You are not worthy of my love or favor. Early in our relationship together, we experienced a drastic business failure that eventually cost us our home and the repossession of our vehicles. Had we "blamed" the other and took our frustrations out on our mate, then our relationship would have suffered great harm and possibly even fatal damage. However, by accepting that all people can and do and will make mistakes in judgment, we were able to start over and build a new life financially together. We were able to go forward and not get stuck in the mire of blame.

Here's a secret. If *you* want acceptance in all aspects of your life, of who you are, emotionally, physically, and as important, sexually, then you have to be accepting of everything your lover is as well. The good and the bad. The great and the mediocre, the strengths and the weaknesses. You give your lover that and your lover will give you the same kind of acceptance. We like to call it the boomerang effect. You throw it out there and it comes right back at you.

Inside of every human being is the most natural craving for complete acceptance. Every one of us desires to let one other person see all we are and be loved anyway. And "all" includes the good, the bad, the sleazy, the sexy, the dirty, the charm, the tenderness, *everything*.

You can't change your mate, but you can change yourself. If you love this person, with all of your heart, then you are willing to make adjustments, you are willing to put into operation a system of checks and balances, if you will. If you know that something really bugs the daylights out of your mate, such as hanging up your wet towels rather than leaving them in a heap on the floor, (maybe it's just simply laziness or a habit that you've had all your life), it's very easy to change the little details in your life, because you want to please the person that you are with. Maybe it's as simple as washing the coffee pot out early enough in the day so that the coffee filter is dry by 9:00 p.m. when you make the coffee and get it ready for the next morning. That's really not a hard thing to do. It doesn't require any inconvenience on your part. It does require a little thought. But then, if you profess to love this other person, you will always be thinking of things that make his or her life easier and better. Remember, it is not all about you.

The point is that, no, you can't change your mate, but if you love your mate, then you can make adjustments in your life that make his or her life easier and we would almost guarantee you that if you do those things for the other person that there will be some pay back. Because when you love a person, honestly and completely, unless they are a completely selfish moron, they are going to respond, because no one can sit back and be loved completely and not love in return. If they can, then perhaps you'd better rethink your reason for being in the relationship to start with.

Remember, we talked about the boomerang effect? It is physically impossible for you to give everything you have inside of yourself, and the other person not respond in kind to you. They will do exactly the same thing back to you. They will give and do and make adjustments. They will make adjustments in all areas of their life. The boomerang effect. It works incredibly well when two people have opened up completely and are being totally honest with everything in their lives, about all the things they like, all the things they don't like. That is when the boomerang effect takes effect. It really is easy and simple, but it is also hard because most of us as human beings can never arrive at that level of trust. We are too selfish to allow the boomerang effect to begin to take effect. But the boomerang effect does exist. We have experienced it. We know it exists. We have never had it in any other relationship prior to this. It took a lot of years and heartaches and tears to learn how to throw the boomerang out there and expect positive results. And yes, it works to the negative as well. If you throw out nothing but anger, strife, jealousy, resentment, then you will get back coldness, hurt, more resentment, etc.

The positive effect starts with giving. Giving is throwing the boomerang away from yourself. In all reality, the boomerang may not come back to you, if you have not thrown it properly. You may lose it. However, what we found, when thrown properly, it always comes back. When it comes back, here's the fun part, it comes back with more force than when you first threw it out there.

So design around the problem that bugs you. Give a little more of yourself. Throw the boomerang and see what happens. In addition to that, what both of you need to understand, is that if you didn't love them, if you didn't care about them, you wouldn't say a word or take any action. If you don't care about someone, why bother? We only "bother" about the ones we genuinely care about.

There are a lot of people in this world who are our associates, or just friends. Most of you can probably count the number of true friends you have on one hand. But most of you probably have a lot of people that you count as associates. You don't try to change your associates. They are who they are and you either choose to be around them or not. Perhaps you choose to be around them for particular things. We have certain friends that are sports fanatics. If we want to go to a ball game, we go with our sports fanatics friends. If we are interested in going to the ballet or talking about chess or playing tennis, we have different friends who share those interests. We choose the ones that are most aligned with what we are doing in deciding who we will be with.

However, the things that happen in your associate's lives don't really deeply impact yours. It doesn't matter one way or the other what happens in their lives, for the most part. They are unimportant to you. You accept them and get on with your own life.

Your friends are another matter. You do care about them and what happens to them. You want them to be successful and have a good life. And you're willing to be honest with them when you see something that perhaps they need to "work on." But you never condemn them. You probably don't "stay on their case." You respect their right to make their own choices and to make their own way in this life. *You accept who they are.*

If you can accept your acquaintances and your friends, why can't you accept your lover as well? You easily accept the failures and foibles of your acquaintances and friends. You accept it when they are "honest" with you about your own shortcomings. You might even have some sort of standing joke between you if you've been friends long enough. But you realize you can't change them and make them over into your own image. They are who they are and that's that.

But you don't have to live with that person. You do have to live with your lover and you are trying to build a perfect relationship. If you weren't, you wouldn't be reading this book. You do realize that when a friend is "honest" with you, they are saying the things they do because they care. Not because they are being mean or cruel or facetious or they are picking or nitpicking or whatever, but they are talking because they care.

If you can hear a friend say things to you about yourself and you don't get angry or upset or depressed, then why would you react that way with your lover? You value the relationship and want it to continue. They know that these are things that you need to correct and you have to be willing to listen. You have to be willing to try to change them and correct them. If you come in from work every day and plop in front of the television while your mate prepares a meal, and your lover voices the sentiment to you that this is upsetting, and your help would be appreciated, then you should act upon that. You could put a TV in the kitchen and watch while you help. It is called sharing. In a truly good relationship you both share not only the fun but the "chores" as well. Make some changes, design around the problem. You can fix anything through design.

You can not change the person that you are in a relationship with. They are who they are because of everything they have done, everything they have been, all the experiences they have had, the way they were raised, who their family members are, everything. You can not change them. In fact, we are talking about several million years of genetic breeding. Lying dormant within your gene pool, within your being, are codes that will dictate who you are, what you will do, how you will do it, what you will become. Are you lazy? Are you hardworking? Are you intelligent? Are you not so intelligent? All these codes were within you at birth. You have no control over these codes. They exist.

Therefore, we go back to the same scenario. You cannot change the person you are with. But, you can design around the problem. Make it easy for them to do what pleases you and help them be able to give you what you need. Do not lay all the responsibility on their shoulders to "change."

Designing around the problem, however, requires thought, desire and intelligence. Do you have that kind of desire and intelligence, to be able to love someone enough to want to change yourself, to learn how to design around a problem? If, as the example cited earlier your spouse, mate, lover, has a bad habit that drives you nuts, of throwing clothes on the floor, then do something that makes it *easy for you and easy for him or her.* Put a box in the closet, put a box at the foot of the bed, put a television in the kitchen. Make some adjustments on your part, to accommodate the things about your mate that you don't like.

The question can't always be "Is it pretty or is it practical?" And the answer can't always be, "If it's practical, don't even think about it." The pretty and the practical can learn to coexist. Some of the most beautiful structures in the world are bridges, but they are indeed extremely practical as well. Believe us, there are places in your life that your mate can't stand, that drive your mate nuts as well. You design around the problems that bug you and your mate will be far more willing to design around the problems of the things that bug him or her. The boomerang effect.

Please bear in mind, through this entire book, we're not saying that a male is better or a female is better. What we are saying is that we are different. Uniquely different. Totally and completely different and it is those very differences that we need to examine. It is those difference that Vicki and I have found were the pinnacle of our strengths.

For example, if you look at females as more forgiving, as having more latitude, this is actually a great gift and strength. The male, if he sees this, and he sees the unconditional loving surrender of the female, he can't help but turn around and surrender back to her. It boomerangs back to the male. It will come right back on you guys. You'll find yourself a slave to her as well. And that is the purest form of love. That is the definition of the purest form of love—when both people are absolute slaves *to each other*.

Part of the aspect of being a slave in love is realizing that what you are talking about here is unconditional love. That's a term that's been bandied about in religion and in self help books and in relationship books for decades. But it is so true that in order to have the kind of relationship that most people want and that people dream about, you have to have a complete acceptance of the other person and to accept them *unconditionally* for who they are and realize that you are not going to change them. If any change is going to occur, it is going to be a result of unconditional love from the both of you.

Change is inevitable throughout life. Life is fluid. And when we say fluid, we mean it is ever changing. Always. A river never flows exactly the same. As it flows it constantly,

constantly eats away at its banks, it constantly uproots trees on its banks. It's always changing.

The same occurs in life with individuals and it also happens in relationships. As time goes by, your relationship will change. Now, how you do that relationship, your honesty, your acceptance, these will determine how your relationship will change. In what direction will it go?

We talked about the wall before and building the wall brick by brick. If you attack each brick at the time that it drops into place and pull it out of the wall and throw it away, then you never have a wall between you. Eventually, if you leave that brick, another will be added and then another, and it will become a wall. This wall will get to the point where you cannot step over it, you cannot crawl over it, and eventually you cannot even see over it.

You have to bear in mind that change is inevitable. It's desirable, actually. If you are not changing, you are dying. So you want to change, but you want to change together. *You want to grow together.* You want to make sure that as you grow, your bond becomes tighter. This begins with the simple steps of trust, honesty and acceptance. Those three factors will guarantee that your growth will continue and it will continue in such a fashion that your love will grow deeper and deeper.

If you do not begin your relationship with trust, honesty and acceptance, then you may unfortunately be destined to find yourself 20 or 30 years down the road and looking across the room and realizing, "I don't even know this man/woman I'm married to. He/she is a total stranger to me." Your lives are not intertwined, but rather are two separate structures standing in the same general area with a brick wall in between. There is nothing to connect you, only something dividing you. And don't think it will be the children or the careers, which will keep you together. Children grow up and leave home. They build their own lives. Careers run out, you will grow old. You will retire some day. What will you have left then if you do not have an intertwined relationship? You will have a separate, lonely life. You will not have the love you desire nor will you be able to share wild, arousing, erotic, mutually satisfying sex.

So how do you do it? How do you accept everything about another human being?

THE CHOICE

▼

The road was so wide and beautiful there,
so easy to trod upon.

Choices so many and easy to make,
it seemed no end would come.

Now I stand and look back and realize
with each step the road grew narrower
and harder to walk, until there were
no more choices to be had.

CHAPTER FOUR

▼

"Eneey, Meeny, Miney, Moe"

Choice. The answer to the question in the previous chapter is as simple as choice. *You make a decision to accept.* Then you stick with that decision. You have already made the decision to be completely honest with one another, about all aspects of your life. To love in truth. Truth first of all about yourself, who you are, what you are, what you want. You must acknowledge all of yourself and be honest with yourself about every aspect of your life. Once you have acknowledged truth, then you must decide what you will do with it.

As human beings, we have been given the capacity to think through issues and make decisions, choices and then to act upon those choices. Accepting your lover and everything about him or her is simply a matter of choice. Take off the blinders, look with honest open eyes, see the truth, then decide what you will do with that truth.

Unfortunately, this is where pride can come in and destroy a budding, growing, open relationship. Will you choose to ignore the truth in order to fit in and be what others want you to be or what society thinks you should be, or will you choose to be truthful to yourself, even if it means your *image* will suffer? Pride is in fact, a destroyer of relationships. Anytime you think to yourself, "I could never reveal that about myself," pride is actually at work. Our fear of losing respect, losing face, prevents us from being as open as we should be. Pride and fear go hand in hand. Our pride will not allow us to be vulnerable and possibly seen as weak. However, if you have laid the ground work, then you can dispense with pride and ego and fear and realize you are accepted and valued.

When you accept a person for who he or she is, you give them respect. Respect for who they are, for the wonderful creature that God created. You respect them for their differences from you as well as their sameness to you.

Let's take a quick look at Webster's again. Respect means to feel or show deferential regard for or esteem for another. It also means to relate or refer to, to show concern. Also, a feeling of appreciative, often deferential regard. The willingness to show consideration or appreciation.

Obviously we all want respect. There's an old song entitled *R-E-S-P-E-C-T.* "Found out what it means to me." Those words are good advice. You want respect. Your lover wants respect. But in the very definition of the word, respect is not something you gain or achieve. It is, in fact, something the other *gives* to you. Some say you can earn it or demand it. We say, no. Respect is something we *freely give one another*. We choose (there's that choice thing again) to respect the other.

We choose to feel or show deferential regard for our lover. We choose to esteem our lover above all others. We choose to be appreciative of who he/she is. We are willing to show consideration for and appreciation for the other.

Does this choice have anything to do with whether your lover is a truck driver or a CEO? Not really. It has more to do with you than with him/her. When you first decided to travel down the road together, at that point, you chose. You made a decision to accept (and thereby respect) the other. If you went into the relationship thinking otherwise, then perhaps you should reexamine your reason for being in the relationship. If you cannot respect who your lover is, if you cannot accept them for the person they are, maybe you need to do some soul searching about what you really want in a mate and a relationship.

That man or woman you're with, came with a whole set of baggage. Some new, some old. But baggage nonetheless. And most people are pretty partial to their own baggage. They don't want your baggage. Their baggage is what makes them who they are. Your baggage is what makes you who you are. That's not to say that the baggage doesn't need to be aired out occasionally.

But true respect says you accept their baggage, mildew and all and love them anyway. Perhaps love them because of that baggage. While it may be true that some baggage is more difficult to deal with than others, all can be dealt with ultimately. Some scars maybe deep and professional help may be required to begin the healing process and unlock those doors. But once that has begun, and the doors are cracked open a bit, then trust your mate as well as the professional, to help you, love you and nurture you.

You might say this respect issue is sort of like "Do unto others what you would have them do unto you." Find out what it is that defines respect to your lover. Be inquisitive. Maybe respect to your lover means picking up after yourself. Maybe it means calling when you're going to be late. Maybe it means not bickering in public (that's a favorite of ours—after all, your dirty laundry is not entertainment for the masses). Whatever it means, usually it's not difficult for you to give that. How hard is it to respect the fact that your lover doesn't like dirty clothes or wet towels left on the floor? What is required of you to show that respect? Simple. Put the clothes in a hamper or hang up the towel. Takes all of about 10 seconds to accomplish on your part, but *shows considerable respect* for the other's feelings. How hard is it to respect the fact that your lover grows concerned when you're late? All that's required of you is a quick phone call—and in today's world of cellular phones, that call can be made from anywhere! And it only takes a moment, but it gains tremendous value in the building of a solid relationship. How hard is it to be considerate of another? And respect and consideration are very closely linked.

Sure, it's easy to say we respect someone who's tough on crime or to respect someone who has built a corporation from zero to a world respected leader in a field or someone who changed the face of politics. We honor and show regard for those who are easily identified by the public as "great." Their achievements garner our respect.

But respect in a truly loving relationship is not the same thing. Our mate will in fact disappoint us at times, either in his/her career, or in the fact that they seem to overlook our needs at times. Yet, we still need to choose, as lovers, to respect and show esteem for our partner. Regardless of their successes or failures. Because the truth of every day life is that there will be more failures than successes. If we only respect our lover when he/she is successful, then we are indeed pretty shallow folks and truly more concerned about self than about the relationship, the "us."

Some of you may even be in a situation where, if the word respect came up in regards to your lover, others would shake their head and not understand what you could possibly respect about him/her. No, your lover may not be a world renowned scientist or glamourous personage. He or she may not be beautiful in the eyes of the world. But you didn't start this relationship with a famous scientist or glamourous person. You started with a computer programmer or secretary or lawyer or waitress or truck driver. You didn't choose to love this person because of what they did. And if you did, then you are more shallow than the person you are in love with and maybe you need to rethink your position, because love is not about a paycheck or prestige or glamour, success or accomplishment.

You chose to love them because of who they are. You chose to respect that he/she is kind, caring, considerate, compassionate. You chose to respect that he/she was a no-nonsense kind of person, that he/she was steady, reliable. Or maybe you chose to love and respect them because they were a little bit wild and crazy. Whatever it was, it should have had very little to do with what they had achieved or what their job title was but much more to do with the kind of person they were.

How many times do you actually just genuinely admire your mate? Admiration is such a key issue. It goes hand in hand with respect.

How many times do you say, I love you? Think about it. Maybe a quick in the morning when you leave for work, "I love you," see you tonight, and that's it.

We suggest you look them in the eye, every single day, five, six times a day, call them on the phone once a day and say, I love you. How many times have you looked at your lover and said I'm glad you're my mate? I can't imagine what my life would be like without you being my mate.

How many times do you say to your partner, I'm glad that I'm your partner and I think you are an incredible person? I love you and the measure of who you are is not in what you do, but it's because of who you are. I love you, I accept you for who you are.

Admiration is absolutely key, because every person needs to be admired. It's like that little child who needs that ego boost that says you did a good job, you tried. Maybe you didn't get it right this time, maybe you failed, maybe you screwed up big time, but that doesn't matter, because you are still an incredible person in my book and I know you are not going to quit or give up. I know you are going to do it again, you are going to try again. And you admire the person that is your partner in your relationship and you let them know they are worthy in your eyes and heart. It may take some practice on your part to learn the art of admiration and practice on your lover's part to learn to accept admiration from you. Some people are uncomfortable accepting compliments from anyone, but genuine admiration most people can learn to accept and eventually appreciate.

You may have to look for things to admire, but if you look, you will find something worthy of praise in your mate. Start with something easy, such as "You are an amazing woman. You are so good at..." fill in the blank. Or, "You are the smartest man I know. You are really good at..." fill in the blank. Look for opportunities to praise your partner. When he remembers to change the oil in the car or have the vehicle serviced, remember to thank him and tell him what a nice, thoughtful person he is for taking care of that chore. When she makes an extra stop on the way home to pick out a movie to share, remember to tell her how thoughtful she is for doing so. Admiration doesn't always have to be about big things. More often than not, simple praise for the small favors you do one another is where you will find reasons to admire your lover. These small praises are in fact, the nuts and bolts of your bridge building.

But, don't admire silently. There is nothing worse than silent admiration. Who gives a rip about silent admiration? It doesn't do anybody any good. So speak up, be honest, accepting, respectful and admiring of your lover, out loud or in writing. By practicing admiration, you may well find it becomes easier to respect as well since you will be looking for things to admire and therefore will find things to respect.

However, truly, the issue of respect cannot be fully addressed without looking at tolerance. They are inextricably tied together.

We all have our standards of what we can accept or tolerate in another person. We tolerate the religious beliefs of others. We don't have to agree with them, but we tolerate them. We allow them their beliefs without prohibiting or opposing them. We in fact, respect the right of others to feel, think, act and believe differently than we ourselves may. Our country was founded on these very principles. In order to find more religious tolerance, thousands and thousands came to a wild, untamed country.

Chances are that when you first got together with your lover, there were some things about him/her which you tolerated and simply accepted or overlooked in the "name of love." Maybe those things are now driving you crazy. If that is the case, you need to look back and let history be the teacher for the future.

Maybe you married a girl (or guy) who is a devout believer and went to church or synagogue or mosque twice a week. At the time, you respected his/her beliefs and in fact may have even been proud of the fact that you were hooked up with a devout person. But now, Saturday evening or Sunday morning rolls around and they're off again and you'd rather they stayed home with you or went to a movie with you. You begin to feel resentment and maybe even bitterness over one of the very things you respected to start with.

Truly, being tolerant of your lover is loving your lover. Is that to say you should tolerate and be silent? No. There is nothing wrong with expressing yourself in an honest, *loving* way about your needs, wants and desires for yourself as well as for the other person.

But again, you cannot change the person you are with. You can only accept them and in some cases, tolerate their foibles and their differences to you. But tolerate them *in love and work for compromise* if possible.

You may say, "But I can't stand the fact that my husband flirts with anything in skirts." Our guess is that was how he caught you to begin with. If he had not been flirtatious and charming, you wouldn't have fallen for him.

Sometimes you simply have to be willing to *forgive* your mate for the things that "make you crazy." You have to allow some leeway for your lover's variation from your own personal standards. You have to recognize and *respect* that your lover's beliefs and practices are different from yours. Tolerance implies that you provide a margin for error or shortcomings. If you want to receive tolerance, it is wise to give it as well. You are not perfect. Why should you expect your lover to be?

It is up to you to realize that one is male and one is female and you are vastly different because of that. Rather than be upset by the differences, rejoice in them. As any man will tell you, men are *gross* creatures when they are amongst their own kind (other men). They will do and say things that are not fit for female company. However, in a loving relationship, that man of yours just might "slip" and behave "naturally." It is up to you as his lover to be tolerant of his natural being and at times rejoice in it because it just might lead to a fun, wild, passionate sexual experience. And it is up to him to realize that some things just might be offensive to his female and to rein in just a bit. In other words, to be tolerant of the fact that she is female. We will make note here, however, that the more compatible two people are, the less there will be to "tolerate" about the other.

All men and all women want to be loved, respected, admired, and yes, tolerated. But sometimes, it seems there are things we just cannot tolerate.

SHARKS

▼

Watch out for the sharks in life,
who tell you what you want to hear
to get you off their backs.
Be it big or small, the sharks in life
will lie and cheat and steal from you,
make promises to you they never mean to keep.

Don't count on the sharks in life,
who if you believe in them,
you'll end up down and out and
holding the bag, all your plans and dreams
nothing but rubble and dust.

The problem is, the sharks in life
look just like you and me,
they're doctors, and lawyers and CPA's,
mechanics and salesmen and barmaids.
The difference is, the sharks in life
have no conscious, have no soul.
Their only purpose in life is to feed-On you.

CHAPTER FIVE

▼

"THE GREEN EYED MONSTER"

Jealousy. Jealousy has no place in a true loving relationship. You do not own the other person. They do not own you. But, you do give yourself freely and willingly to that other person and that other person has given themselves freely and willingly to you. Being jealous of the fact that they may see another person and think that other person is attractive is a waste of energy and a waste of time and harmful to your relationship. Until at such time as your mate loses his or her sight, he or she will always see beauty and attractiveness in another human being. There is absolutely nothing wrong with expressing appreciation for the beauty of the human form, be it male or female. Both should be able to voice that in front of the other without being offensive or offended. In other words, openness and honesty.

Let's look for a moment at the meaning of jealousy. It can have both a good and a bad meaning. The "bad" meaning is the one that is most often applied in a relationship. Most people who display jealousy in a relationship are indeed fearful or wary of losing their place in that relationship, afraid of losing the affection of the other. Why? Because either trust, truth, honesty, acceptance or tolerance are missing from the relationship.

However, the proper use of jealousy in a relationship is one of being *vigilant in guarding* that relationship, and to be intolerant of disloyalty or infidelity in your mate. All these are actually good "jealousy." They protect and guard your relationship. The negative kind of jealousy has no place in a loving relationship, and indeed will not have a place in a truth based, honesty based, completely open relationship.

Love is not a competition. This person loves you. This person cares about you. If not, they would not be with you. Being jealous (in the "bad" sense) is detrimental to your relationship. It is a bunch of bunk. Movies and books and television, etc. are full of bunk about this type of jealousy. "Well, I'm going to make him jealous because he looked at another woman, so I'm going to flirt with another man and I'm going to make him jealous so that he will come running back to my arms."

More often than not, that strategy is going to backfire and what you're going to have on your hands is trouble or your worst fears confirmed. This is the boomerang with a negative effect.

From the male's point of view, jealousy exists for a purpose. Go back in time, back into our past and you will find that reason. Jealousy born out of fear is a "modern man" term and usage. It's also a term that has been around for hundreds of years as a term we put on a jealous male or a jealous female. But, prior to that, back several thousand years, jealousy was what motivated a male to protect his territory. He jealously guarded his domain, his territory, and his property because he *valued* it. His territory would have been whatever area he deemed was necessary to help in his survival and help him provide for the family he had. His family could have been several females. It could have been one female, depending on the area and the culture. It makes no difference what part of the planet you talk about, from Eskimos to South American Indians to African natives. Jealousy was a motivational factor for the male. It caused him to make a move and to protect what he deemed to be his, what he owned.

Let's take a closer look. In reality, is a female ever really "owned" by a male? If you think about man's past, the answer is yes. He really owned her until he was defeated in combat or died. At that time, she became the property of the victor. That's how it was several thousand years ago, during the early days of man's walk upon this planet.

Genetically, that has not changed. In our minds, genetically speaking, we are still that way. We still think and feel that way. We *own* things. Today, however, man cannot act upon those feelings like he did in those more primitive times. Now, we like to think of ourselves as more sophisticated. But man's feelings are not sophisticated. Man is still at his base, a primal creature. We love. We protect. We serve. That is our purpose. That is how we were designed.

Jealousy is not necessarily a bad thing. It is only bad if it is ungoverned and misused, if it gets in the way of common sense. Jealousy is not a tool to be used against your lover. It is a tool to be used to *protect your lover and your relationship*. To set out to "make your lover jealous" is a destructive urge. Acting upon that urge will be destructive and detrimental to a healthy relationship.

However, jealously guarding your relationship from the intervention of others, who do not have the best interest of the relationship at heart, is a well-motivated use of the natural instinct found in all of the human species. Let us give you an example of good jealously at work in a relationship.

Let's say a man and woman are out at a dance club. The woman leaves for a moment to go to the restroom to freshen up. While she is gone, another female comes over and tries to garner the attention of the man. Now, if he's a normal man, he probably will respond to her attentions at least to some extent. Either that, or he can be entirely rude and obnoxious to the other woman and she will get the message pretty clearly. But for the sake of argument, let's say that he is a pretty decent guy, and being rude is not something he practices, particularly with women. Okay, the wife comes out of the restroom and sees this other woman paying undue attention to her man and he is in fact responding to her attentions. The wife has two choices here. She can either say "well, that rat" (meaning her husband) and immediately look around for a likely candidate on which to turn her considerable charms in an effort to "make her husband jealous" and thereby gain his attention once again. Or, she can smile sweetly, walk over to the two people, extend her hand to the "strange" female and introduce herself as his wife and then pay him an incredible compliment and let the other woman know that she can certainly see why she would choose to flirt with him.

In the first scenario, she may succeed in getting his attention, but it will most likely be a negative and possibly even angry reaction. At that point, they are both off down the "bad jealousy" road and the battle is about to begin. In the second scenario, she displays her jealousy in the proper direction, and sets off a good chain of events. Unless the other woman is a complete idiot, she will get the message very quickly that this man is well spoken for, and she will go her way. The wife has just jealously defended her territory, but in the process, not only did she not set off negative events in the relationship, but she even built the relationship up by *admiring her mate* at the same time. And as we said earlier, everyone loves to be admired and appreciated. Admiration is a very fine way to diffuse a potentially bad situation and completely disarm the "enemy."

This scenario could easily be reversed. The man leaves to go get drinks. When he returns, he finds another man "invading his territory." He has two choices. He can display his macho-ness and go punch the other guy in the nose, and probably embarrass the female, or he can rein in his natural aggression just a bit, taking into consideration the fact that if he is arrested or thrown out of the place, then she is either left alone and at the mercy of anyone who might wish to attempt to gain her favor, or she may leave with him but be completely embarrassed that she was in the midst of a head butting contest. Not that females don't enjoy being fought over. They do. However, in today's day and age, there is another way to diffuse the situation. He could, rather than punching the guy in the face, and risking not only arrest, but pain as well, simply walk up, put the drinks down and say, "I see you've met my wife. Beautiful woman, isn't she?" Then put his arm around her to let it be known that this is "his" and not public property. Most men will generally get the message and back off. And the woman not only was spared embarrassment, but also complimented as well.

This kind of good jealousy can only be achieved if you have built the bridges of trust, truth, honesty, acceptance, respect and tolerance.

If jealousy plays a healthy role in a relationship, what role do revenge, retaliation, spite, vengeance and hypocrisy (lying) have in a healthy relationship?

EMPTY POCKETS

My pockets are way too full
with little things and some big stuff, too.

The hurts I placed in there
have cluttered my pockets with so much,
until the strings that tied my heart to yours,
the stars that fell with each harsh word,
the flowers that wilted with each cold shoulder,
have gotten too tangled to keep them
straight anymore.

It's time to empty my pockets
and throw the pain away.

For if I don't, the end will be the same
as once before, and soon I'll need
a closet with the stoutest door.

CHAPTER SIX

▼

"The War Museum"

Revenge, retaliation, spite, vengeance, and hypocrisy have absolutely no place in your relationship. Then you may ask why would we even bother to include a discussion of these things in a book on relationships? The answer is simple. In far too many cases, these are practiced by the partners in a relationship and always with a negative outcome to the relationship.

We have seen on countless occasions people engaged in revengeful or vengeful acts against their partner. One gets hurt by some action of the other and that one then decides to "get even" and inflict an equal or similar kind of hurt on the other. When this happens, the demolition crew has just arrived and the bridges are being torn down rather than built. The walls are now being erected between the two supposedly loving people.

The old expression "cut off the nose to spite the face" comes to mind. In a relationship, spite and revenge and vengefulness more often than not lead to damage to both parties involved. The one who is retaliating usually winds up just as hurt as the one retaliated against.

The emotional pain that we suffer when our lover hurts us is far different from physical pain. The pain of childbirth or the pain of a laceration or broken arm are fairly easy to forget and overcome with time. With emotional pain, however, most people tend to subvert it and attempt to stick it in the back of our mind. We try to sweep it under the rug and pretend that it never happened, that it doesn't exist, and therefore, we don't have to deal with it. Unfortunately, though we may have been able to tell ourselves we overreacted or blew things out of proportion or even blame ourselves for the infliction of the emotional pain, when we try to avoid dealing with it, it simply festers and grows and eventually rears its ugly head.

With emotional pain, you must deal with it openly and honestly with your mate as soon as possible. The more immediate to the situation the better. Far better to deal with the resentment and anger while it's still a relatively small issue than to wait and allow the festering to start and eventually grow into an explosive mess. That mess will someday rupture like the nasty boil that it is and become a weapon for the war museum.

If you allow resentment to grow and fester you have just added a brick to the wall between you and your lover, or a piece of armament has been added to the battle gear. The more little resentments you allow to fester, the more bricks you lay and the higher the wall becomes.

There are of course, positive and negative ways to deal with the emotional hurts that occur between even the most loving of couples. The negative means are through spiteful acts, revenge, vengeance, etc. For example, let's say your mate embarrassed you by yelling at you in public or in front of friends. At the time, you were mortified and perhaps unable to respond immediately. But that hurt is growing and festering inside and the mind starts to think of ways to "get even" and inflict the same or similar hurt on the other. A spiteful person might inflict his/her revenge by attempting to publicly humiliate the other through remarks about the others sexual prowess or job failure or something similar.

The problem with this scenario is that although you may have achieved your goal of returning the favor of embarrassment upon your mate, you have in fact, made yourself look petty and small in the eyes of those in front of whom you exacted your revenge. Yes, you may have gotten your revenge. However, what you have done is taken a piece of your own soul away and more importantly, you have destroyed the one thing that you sought in the beginning of this relationship. Oneness. Back in chapter one the issue of trust was discussed. When you stooped so low to go after revenge, you destroyed trust. You may win the day. You may win that battle, but in the end you will lose the war because trust has been destroyed and no longer will your lover look at you or trust he/she can go out in public with you and feel comfortable knowing that you are not going to bash or humiliate them. Trust has been destroyed by the petty emotion of revenge. You never want to destroy trust. You must have complete trust in your mate, always. They must have complete trust in you. Far better to have perhaps placed a quiet hand on your partner's arm and whispered in his/her ear that very moment or as soon as you were alone together to calmly let the other one know you were hurt, how and why. No recriminations. No accusations. Just simple, quiet, honest truth based on trust, love, acceptance and tolerance.

Relationships are not about getting even or keeping score. They are not about revenge or competition. One of the biggest mistakes people make in a relationship is they start keeping score of who did what to whom and when and how many times. In fact, they are stacking brick upon brick and working on the wall and adding battle swords and spears to the war chest. When you are hurt, you store that away and save it for the next time, so that when you have an argument in the future, you can go running back to your war chest and bring out this little piece of something and say, well, but you did this and you did that and you hurt me.

When it comes to relationships, the war chest has no place. You must get rid of it completely. If you don't, here's the scenario: You get into an argument and one runs off to his/her war chest and drags out "the night that you came in at 3 a.m." and then the other runs to their war chest and comes back with "what about the time I called and called and you weren't home till 8 p.m. when you were supposedly just out to lunch with friends." And the battle begins. Each will run back and forth to the war chest and grab the next weapon, each one more deadly than the last, then come back out and do battle with it and the war goes on and on. In the end you are literally screaming at one another about the other's faults and shortcomings. No one wins. Both lose. And both get hurt even more.

What you must realize is that every one of those weapons are actually a brick in the wall that is being constructed between the two of you rather than a girder in the bridge you want to build.

What can you do to stop the war before it begins? When a problem or hurt occurs, deal with it. Get it out into the open, the sooner the better. Sit down, talk about it. Yell if need be. Cry. It doesn't matter. Don't stop until that brick has been removed from the wall and smashed to the ground. When you finish, agree that the brick is gone. If you are not far enough along in your relationship to talk openly, then try writing it down, in a loving way, explaining how you were hurt and why. Do not use anger as a tool. Use love as your weapon.

You can not have revenge in a relationship. It has no place. There is no purpose for it. It's actually a waste of your energy and a waste of your thoughts. World wars have been started in the name of revenge. Why would you believe for a moment that your relationship could survive this petty emotion? What do you have to have revenge for? This is somebody you love. This is somebody that you chose to spend all of the days remaining on this planet with. Why would you want to take out revenge against them? Think about it, it's just a waste of time. Once you realize this, you understand revenge has no place in your life. It has no purpose. It causes you to think unnecessarily about negatives rather than positives. It causes you to look for ways to hurt and destroy rather than to heal and build.

There will be another day as long as you are committed to the relationship. And if both people come to the relationship with that attitude, then it's so much easier to work through things and work out whatever the problem is because you are committed to the fact that you have a tomorrow. There is going to be another day, because you are both committed to the relationship. Remember, a harsh word begets anger, but a soft answer turns away wrath. If your mate yells at you, your natural reaction is probably to scream back and thereby set off a sequence of even more harshness and anger, even more potential for wounding and being wounded. Diffuse the situation with a soft, sincere reply.

As for lying, we have extensively discussed that in a previous chapter. However, remember, "Oh, what a tangled web we weave when first we practice to deceive." That truly is an excellent reminder that lying and hypocrisy have absolutely no place n a relationship. The first time you choose to tell even a small lie, you are in danger of needing to lie again and again in order to cover the first lie, until you eventually have such a tangled mess even you can't keep it straight. At that point, energy which should be going towards building is now wasted on covering your sin.

So what do all these things we have discussed so far, truth, trust, honesty, acceptance really have to do with anything? As we said, all are an integral part of a good relationship. But what makes a relationship great?

THE BOOK

I'm a book you never had to read,
for you wrote the lines
and know the story as your own.

We've lived our lives with others together,
yet always alone.

They did not know how to use the secret key
to unlock the doors to our hearts,
shut against years of pain and judgment,
always falling short of their mark.

Right and wrong were never clear—
our ears could not hear their chorus of lies.

Deep inside our music played
the song of two hearts,
bound before first daybreak or evening set—
we tried and failed at the miserable task
of fitting into their life's plans—
too strictured for us to bear alone.

In your eyes I see, when you look at me,
no condemnation nor negative thought.
Only love lives in our two hearts,
made as one by creator before time began
and life took over to cloud our minds
and shackle our souls by societies threads,
where neither fit in nor followed the rules
laid down by some unseen hand.

In solitude we fought our hearts and lost,
time and again, until our wills were crushed
within the walls of convention's call.
Our language all our own,
understood only by us,
for we wrote the book
our two hearts finally read.

CHAPTER SEVEN

▼

"Peas and Carrots or Two Peas In A Pod"

The old saying is that opposites attract. While that is true, we have found that people who are too opposite from each other often run into more problems than two who are extremely compatible with each other. That is not to say that differences are not inherent in a relationship. Differences can indeed be complimentary. After all, the first and biggest difference may be that you are male and female. Feminine and masculine. We are not saying that all relationships of value involve a man and a woman. What we are saying is that there will be a "feminine" personality and a "masculine" personality. You can put whatever physical parameters on that you wish. We are not here to define the physical makeup of your relationship.

Opposites do indeed attract and can in fact, sometimes form a mutually satisfying, compatible relationship. However, it often is the very things that are opposite about one another that over the long haul of a relationship, throughout the long bridge building process, get in the way and cause the most problems.

The more you have in common with your lover, the easier it will be to build the bridges you will need to cross all the rivers that will come along. The more you are capable of existing or performing in harmonious, agreeable and congenial combination with one another, the easier your relationship will be to build and grow.

In the ideal sense of a relationship, the two of you should be able to be "integrated" into one to work cohesively as a whole unit, rather than disparate units working separately for different purposes. The desire should be for orderly, efficient integration and operation with the other with no or few modifications required. The more you have in common, the more you see life in a like manner, the easier this joining will be.

We are not saying that a relationship of opposites cannot work. Many do. We are saying that there are plenty of problems in a relationship to deal with and that the more common ground you can find, the easier creating the kind of relationship you desire will become.

When two people are trying to build a great relationship and they are extremely opposite from each other, the common ground is harder to find. For example, if one loves football and the other hates it, then the one who loves it will probably go off with friends to enjoy the game leaving the other alone. Or if one loves the opera or ballet and the other despises it, then one will inevitably have to enjoy that alone or with others rather than enjoying it together.

These are of course, very simple examples. The point is, the more areas of differences there are in a relationship, the more time will be spent apart from the relationship and in the company of others. And those others may or may not always have the best interest of your relationship at heart.

If one is a strict and stern disciplinarian and the other is very lenient and forgiving, there will be friction when it comes to the issues of how to raise a child. There will be tension because the one who is the disciplinarian will feel the need to always be strict and never feel he/she has the opportunity to be forgiving because their partner never disciplines. If you are not compatible and in fact are very opposite from one another in this area, then the one who is the disciplinarian will probably be even more so than they might normally have been because they feel the entire burden rests with them. If you are very compatible in this area, then the responsibility is more evenly divided and no one has to be tough and hard all the time. Also, on this particular matter, what can and often does happen is the child is the one who really loses. The child loses the opportunity to feel the same love from both parents because one of the parents is always hard and tough and the child will probably grow up with a complex or "hate attitude" towards the harsher parent.

This happens all too often, because humans are not patient and we don't take the time to properly search for our life mate. We get tired of being alone and we settle. Or we bow to societal or peer pressure to be in a relationship and we accept less than what we truly desire and in fact really need. And the more areas where you are not compatible, then the more chances for trouble.

The more differences there are in a relationship, the easier for wedges to be driven between the two of you and the harder it is to build bridges. In a sense, every difference is a potential brick in the wall. For example, couples who are perhaps not extremely compatible, but who are together for a variety of reasons, spend a lot of time apart from each other. And some of that time, outside of work, is in situations that open the door wide for invasion. The "ladies night out" scenario is a good example. A couple are together, but not completely compatible, and so once a week, the girls get together and go to a bar for drinks and dancing. She is in imminent danger. Why? Because the very fact that she is there indicates some restlessness in her, and some unsatisfactory aspect to her relationship. After a couple of drinks, her guard is let down and she is "fair game" for anyone to attempt to persuade her to spend even more time apart from her relationship. Multitude of affairs have begun just from this type of scenario.

The other side of this is a situation we experienced early in our relationship. Gil's brother invited him to a game cook off but explicitly said it was "guys only." Gil chose not to go because he didn't want to come home and say to me, "Hey, baby, you should have been there. It was great." Especially early in a relationship, it is critical to spend as much time together as possible. That's how you learn each other. The more time spent apart in the company of others, the less time you have to devote to building your bridges. But, the less compatible you are, the less likely you are to want to spend all your time together. It needs to be said here that it is more than compatibility at this point. It is truly about love and that you would rather be with your mate than with anyone else on earth. If you are very compatible, then your mate can be not only your wife, lover, husband, partner, but your best friend as well. The more compatible you are, the better friends you will be.

You must come to a meeting of the minds very early in your relationship about a vast array of issues. God, religion, rearing children, careers and so much more. Any issue, large or small, is easier to deal with if you are of a common mind and a common purpose. In the end, it boils down to being patient and waiting and searching for the right person for yourself. And in so doing, you will have not only a vibrant, loving relationship, but also a peaceful one as well. There will be very little conflict. We all have enough strife and turmoil to deal with in our day to day lives with work, careers, family demands, etc., that we certainly don't want conflict on the love front. Your love relationship should be your sanctuary from the world. It should be the place you can come to with absolute assurance that you will find peace and harmony. You can unwind, release the stress, relax and enjoy the presence of your best friend as well as your lover, all rolled into one. This kind of situation allows you to recharge fully so you can go out again and again and tackle the worries of your "outside life." The more compatible you are, the more of a safe haven your relationship will be against the forces which would attempt to prevail against you.

What does this mean? Does it mean that if you are not alike in all things that you cannot be happy? Absolutely not. It means you may have to work a bit harder at your relationship than the couple who is exceptionally compatible in a multitude of areas. You might say, they have an advantage going in.

And sex is a huge issue when it comes to compatibility. If one is outgoing, extroverted even, when it comes to sex and the other believes it is a "bad" or "dirty" act, then there are bound to be problems. The relationship cannot possibly be as fulfilling as if both were of the same mind. Hopefully that mind is that sex is a good and beautiful thing to be enjoyed fully by both partners. Unfortunately, if the issue of compatibility is overlooked or deemed not as important as other things, i.e., money, security, etc., then the sexual experience within the relationship will not be a good and beautiful thing. It will be a duty. One more chore to deal with in a list of already too many. If you are not of the same mind when it comes to sex and sexual pleasure, one of you is going to get frustrated sooner or later. And frustration will eventually lead to action.

Sex is a powerful motivator for individuals. If it were not, then magazines, television, music, none would use it as a means of "selling" us on anything. But it is in fact, the primary weapon of the media when attempting to convince us that we must have this car or that kind of vacation. If you sell yourself short in this realm of your relationship in regards to compatibility, you are eventually headed for trouble. If you love sex and sexual pleasure and your mate is ho-hum about it, then you will eventually tire of trying to enjoy fulfilling sex with your mate and possibly may start to look outside the relationship to find what you need. Or, if the one who is so-so about sex gets tired of "always being pestered" to have sex, that one is likely to become bitter, resentful, possibly angry and certainly an unpleasant person to be around.

An additional concern here for the one in the relationship who really enjoys the sexual aspect is that the longer they do without out it, the more frustrated they can become, the more sex will be desired, craved and eventually sought after. This opens the door for affairs and/or one night stands, which obviously will ultimately harm and possibly destroy the relationship. So, it matters not if you both adore the sexual aspect of your love, or can take it or leave it. What matters is that you are of the same mind about sex and its place in your relationship. Aside from financial difficulties, problems in the sexual arena are one of the leading causes of relationships going awry.

Early in a relationship, you need to talk, talk, talk and open the doors inside each of you in order that you may know and your mate may know, who you really are. You might look at it as walking down a long, dark hallway. Your mate represents this hallway. In this long hallway, there are many, many doors. Behind each of those doors is something you need to know about your mate. These doors are locked, some from the inside and some from the outside. It is your job to unlock those doors that you can unlock. And to your surprise, you may find that within those rooms, are the doors to the other rooms which you could not access from the hallway. By unlocking these doors, this enables you to find more and more areas of commonality and gives you a framework to build your bridges upon.

No, you don't have to be exactly alike. That really would be boring. As stated earlier, there are fundamental differences which involve feminine and masculine. Men and women will look at life in very different ways. However, values and beliefs, and hopes and dreams and aspirations, are similar in male and female alike. All need and desire love, companionship, acceptance. All want truth and honesty in a relationship. All want and need to be forgiven for their faults. All need to grow and develop and become the total human being they were designed to be. All need for their lover to be tolerant of their flaws. And in the end, everyone wants to be satisfied sexually. In other words, everyone needs a little grace now and then. You can be extremely compatible in myriad ways, however also strikingly different in some areas, but those areas should generally compliment the weakness or strength of the other, therefore taking the burden. Be complimentary to each other as much as you are compatible with each other.

The male personality will most likely be the more dominant in a relationship. The female will most likely be the more submissive. Is this good or bad? Neither. It is genetics, pure and simple. We were created male and female. In order to achieve a complete relationship, this is one area we simply have to acknowledge and accept. We are different as creatures. We have different purposes. The male is genetically configured to provide for and protect. The female is configured genetically to nurture and give care to others. Is this saying that there are no males who are nurturing and giving? Is it saying that there are no females who can provide for and protect what she cares about? Of course not.

However, one set of characteristics will be far stronger in each individual. The need and desire to provide and protect will be stronger than the desire to give nurture and vise versa.

Part of the beauty of the kind of relationship we have been talking about thus far is that we accept the fundamental differences in the masculine and feminine and in fact, embrace those differences, while jointly searching for areas of compatibility.

But in truth, when it comes to sexual pleasure, a celebration of the differences is to be desired. Let male be male and female be female. And enjoy sex in all its fullness.

Sex

▼

Sex with the same man is like
slipping into an old shoe,
    comfortable, undemanding,
        the grooves and hollows known.

Sex with a stranger is like
dressing in red from head to toe,
    daring, exciting,
        the thrill of taking a chance.

Sex with a lover is like
fireworks on the fourth of July,
    explosive, passion,
        filled with light and sound.

So, I'll cherish red and make believe
    it's a stranger who is my lover.

For one night, or maybe two.

CHAPTER EIGHT

▼

"FLIGHTS OF FANCY"

You've opened doors and found doors within rooms leading to other rooms. Now, let your imagination take flight in your relationship with one another. After all, what is fantasy but the creative imagination or unrestrained fancy? Fantasy is an imagined event or sequence of mental images, like a daydream, usually fulfilling a wish or psychological need. When we fantasize, we portray events or actions in our minds.

Fantasy has a very definite place in a healthy, loving, trusting relationship. Through fantasy and the sharing of our fantasies, we learn about our mate and even more importantly, we learn about ourselves. To explore fantasy with our lover is to reveal who we are, or perhaps who we would like to be for at least a little time. Most of us don't want to live in that fantasy forever, but we do want to explore it. We want to explore alternate realities, alternate lives and lifestyles. When shared with your lover, your fantasy life can become a bridge to a rich and even more meaningful relationship. When hidden from your lover, fantasies can become stumbling blocks or walls to a fulfilling relationship.

Again, all the previous things we've talked about come into play when you begin dealing with the fantasy aspect of your relationship. You must have a bond of trust, truth, acceptance, tolerance, admiration. There can be no urge for retaliation, no hurt feelings because of what the other's fantasy maybe. Believe us, when it gets to the fantasy aspect of your life, if you don't have a bridge of trust built, you have no way to cross the river that lies between the two of you, between the fantasy and the reality of maybe of fulfilling that fantasy. Without that trust that you have built over a period of time, you cannot do it.

If you don't take care of each other's fantasies, it is highly likely they will be fulfilled somewhere else. Sooner or later each of you will seek an outlet for your fantasy. Or maybe you will live them in your head, always wishing you could indulge the reality of them at least once. Daydreaming will become a favorite pastime. You may even spend years and years with your lover, in bed "making love" but never be truly focused on him/her because you don't feel you can really open up. Or, perhaps you will suppress your fantasies and just be miserable because you are denying a part of who you are. You may begin to bash your mate behind his/her back, you may start to constantly find fault with him/her because you resent the fact you can't be open and honest and you feel you have to hide something. Eventually you may wind up either cheating on your mate or you may even end up divorcing.

But you will at some point attempt to fulfill those dreams and fantasies. To do this, you may live several different lifestyles attempting to fulfill those fantasies and dreams, hiding financial resources, lying. You may go to work as Mr. Conservative Lawyer, or doctor, dressed appropriately, talking appropriately, but at night, you are cruising the gay bars or you will be chasing topless dancers. Or, you may pretend to be out with friends for lunch when in fact, you are cruising looking for erotic, "nasty" sex with a stranger. You are living a double life. We say that is unnecessary. You don't have to do that. You can find everything you want right within your mate if you are both willing to give and trust, be honest, accepting, tolerant, forgiving and withhold anger, jealousy, retaliation and resentment.

What is the definition of a fantasy? Fantasy in a relationship is something that most people keep to themselves. They don't share it with anyone else. Oh, they may talk to their girlfriends about it or a guy may talk to his buddies about it, because it is non-threatening to do so in this way, and it may even garner a few oohs and ahhs. But no real risk is involved. No danger to the relationship. However, you don't tell your partner about that fantasy. A guy won't go in and tell his wife, man I've got this fantasy of watching you with another woman. Why? Because she'd probably freak out and go through the roof if the groundwork of trust, truth, honesty, acceptance, tolerance, etc., has not been previously laid. And a woman consequently won't come in and say that she's got a fantasy of watching him with another woman or she's got a fantasy of being with two guys at one time because there is no trust and mutual acceptance.

Fantasies will possibly be the hardest issue to deal with, because they deal with those secret lives and secret desires. Remember, we talked earlier about having different people that make up you? All the different characters that make up a single, individual, unique person will be involved in the fantasy aspect of your relationship.

One of the characters in there may be the rock star that likes to hang out at the rock and roll clubs or maybe he wants to go to a country and western bar or maybe even hang out at the topless clubs. After all, one of the main reasons why men frequent topless clubs is because of fantasy…the desire to see beautiful women dancing naked for him and perhaps he is afraid to share that wish with his lover. Or perhaps he did once upon a time ask his wife to dance topless for him in the privacy of the home and she flat out refused. He is now looking elsewhere to have that desire fulfilled.

Whatever is inside of you, whatever those fantasies are, you have to be able to explore them with your mate and your mate has to be able to accept them for what they are. This is not something you want to do all the time and it is not a reflection of anyone's inadequacies. They are just simply something you want to explore and have fun with.

You want to pretend. You want to play make believe. Just like you did when you were younger, when you were a kid and you used to play doctor or GI Joe or Sgt. Striker or Barbie and Ken. It's no different now that you are an adult. You are just doing it in an adult atmosphere, but remember, with adult emotions at stake.

Fantasy is something that must be dealt with in a healthy relationship. You have to look into each other's life and be honest enough to talk about what those fantasies are. You may be the kind of couple who have to go get a couple of shots of tequila before you'll start opening up and talking about your fantasies. By all means, go buy a bottle of Curevo Gold, go home, sit down, slam back as many as you need, until both of you can start talking about your deepest fantasies. No matter how sick and twisted they may seem to you. No matter how exotic or strange they may seem on the surface. It makes no difference. *Remember they are fantasies*, a departure from what you both acknowledge as reality. And your partner has fantasies as well that may feel just as strange to them, but in truth are no more so than your own. You must know about them and share them if you want a truly fulfilling and healthy relationship. And you must trust in the other person to accept them for what they are. *Fantasies*. They are make believe. You might be surprised to find that person, your mate, will actually start trying to find ways to fulfill a fantasy, make it become a reality for you.

Because fantasy, in the very nature of the word itself, means a divergence from reality. Everyone has a hard enough time in the day to day existence of our lives paying the bills, taking care of the kids, working for a boss we despise, doing a job we are not totally happy with. That's reality. And every one of us deals with reality day after day, hour by hour, month by month, and we do it, because that is what we do, because it's the responsible, expected thing to do. It's the "right thing to do."

Fantasy is where we can diverge from reality. The beautiful thing about diverging from reality within a relationship with someone you trust completely, who accepts you completely, is that both of you know there is safety within your relationship and you can explore your fantasies, your secret desires without fear of reprisal.

Maybe you want to pretend to be a rock star or some famous person or you want to be able to pretend that you are an exotic dancer or a model. You can within the bounds of your relationship in safety, explore your fantasies without fear of reprisal, or recrimination or breaking the law or having to go behind someone's back and sneak around to do it. You can find tremendous joy in exploring your fantasies together.

The reason it is so important your mate know about the fantasy part of your life is the fantasies we have are part of who and what we are. Fantasies make up an integral part of our lives. And to deny they exist, to pretend you don't have fantasies, is to deny part of who you are. There is not anything healthy in denying part of who you are. After all, had it not been for fantasy and flights of fancy, we might never have walked on the moon or sent a mission to Mars.

There may be some out there who would say, well, yeah, but what if my mate's fantasy is to go out and rob or rape or kill or maim somebody? If that's the case, then definitely you need to be getting some serious professional help. We are discussing sexual fantasies and their place in a healthy, loving, trusting, caring, intimate relationship.

By not telling your mate and sharing your fantasies, what you are in fact doing, is lying to them. You are lying to yourself as well. You are committing a double lie. We talked about truth and honesty earlier and how important it is in relationships. This is another issue where truth and honesty must shine through. You have to be completely honest about it. If you don't, you're lying. There is no other way to look at it.

We will say that you may find the fantasy part, putting them forth to your mate, letting them know about your fantasies, could be really difficult in the beginning, because you are just starting out on this pathway of trust and honesty and you don't know how much to trust. You don't realize yet you have to trust with everything. It's going to be difficult at first, but after a while, a year or two down the road, if you have been building your bridges and opening your doors in all areas, those fantasies will be easier to acknowledge and they'll start being fun in the way fantasies were meant to be enjoyed in your relationship with each other. You will actually learn to have fun with them. She'll have fun going out and buying the clothes that you want her to wear on a particular evening to fulfill a fantasy or you'll have fun putting an evening together where you fulfill her fantasy.

Attempting to fulfill another's fantasy does not mean you will perform it to the letter, at least not in the beginning. If her fantasy is to be with two men at once and you are not comfortable with that, then improvise. Wear two different costumes and "be two different kinds of man." Or buy a dildo to use while lovemaking. Use your imagination. Be creative and you will find the means to explore the fantasies of your lover within the bounds you are both comfortable with. If his is to see you with another woman and you "just can't do it," then come up with a compromise. You might consider going to a topless bar and get a dancer to dance for *you*, the female, and in that way at least fulfill a part of his fantasy.

In the beginning it may be hard. It may be very, very difficult for you to open up. That's normal. Just understand it's all a part of the process but it will get easier. "Practice makes perfect."

The funny thing about fantasies we have discovered is that once a fantasy has been fulfilled, then it is no longer a "fantasy" and therefore no longer fits into the realm of "diverging from reality." It is true that some fantasies maybe the kind you want to fulfill over and over for a long period of time. Others will be a one time only affair and once done, will never come up again as a desire. Curiosity does not always kill the cat. Sometimes it satisfies it.

For example, I once had a lovely fantasy of having my lover come home and find a trail of red rose petals strung across the floor, leading into the bedroom, where more rose petals were scattered on the bed and I was lying there in a very sexy outfit waiting to be ravished. Of course, soft music was playing and the candles were lit. This particular fantasy was one I could fulfill myself, and in fact, had to orchestrate myself. I bought a dozen red roses and after lighting candles and setting the music on just the right CD, I scattered the roses from front door to bedroom. I then dressed in my slinkiest, sexiest outfit and waited on the bed. When my lover arrived, he was extremely pleased and more than eager to ravish me. We had wonderful, fun sex. But the reason we will never forget that fantasy and probably will never attempt it again is because of the aftermath. The next day, when cleaning up the red rose petals, we discovered to our dismay, they had left pink stains all over the carpet everywhere one had been stepped on! So, it is a good idea to think your fantasy through completely, lest you get something you didn't bargain for when it's all said and done.

Remember, also that not all fantasies have to be complex or complicated to still satisfy a desire you may have harbored for a long time. It might be something as simple as having champagne and strawberries on Christmas morning while sitting naked in front of the fireplace. Or perhaps you want to go to a nude beach and run around completely naked in front of total strangers. This is not necessarily a sexual fantasy, but it is a fantasy nonetheless if it is something you want to do but have never done. One word of advice here, however. Nude beaches are not what you might think, filled with heavenly, young, nubile bodies. On the contrary, you will more than likely find that the others there are simply quite comfortable with their bodies, in whatever shape they may be in.

One of men's more popular fantasies is the "quickie" or "nooner," hard, fast, hot, animal sex that's over in a matter of minutes. Some women enjoy these encounters as well and are eager and willing to participate or even initiate. The secret here is spontaneity and going with the flow of things. If it feels right, then go for it. After all, not every sexual joining needs to be nor should it be a long drawn out affair.

Another popular fantasy of both men and women is having sex in an unusual place. "The Mile High Club," for example, provides the thrill but be aware of the difficulties. It's a public place (airplane or jet). The area is likely to be tight and confined (the restroom), and there maybe others waiting before you finish your tryst, so obviously there's a potential for embarrassment.

For those of you who might want to look into "toys" to assist in the role playing of a fantasy, there are many places these items can be purchased. In larger areas, you might try looking in the yellow pages under lingerie shops. Some of these carry a wide variety of not only erotic clothing, but also a selection of toys as well as lotions, creams, lubricants, and the like. For those who do not live in a larger metropolitan area or for those who are not comfortable actually going into or out of this type of establishment, then there are catalogues available with a assortment of great gizmos: Good Vibrations, (800) 289-8423; The Xandria Collection (800) 242-2823; Adam and Even (800) 274-0333; Eve's Garden (800) 848-3837. All these are reputable businesses that ship catalogues and merchandise with the utmost of discretion. Even the most shy consumer can be comfortable and not feel intimidated shopping in this manner.

One other thing to keep in mind when dealing with the fantasy aspect of your life and relationship is that most fantasies that individuals have don't always involve their actual partner, but rather involve someone else. This is perfectly normal and does not in any way mean that your partner doesn't love you or want you or that you can't in fact help him/her realize their fantasy.

Take your time and enjoy the fantasy aspect of your life together. Get to know one another on a deeper, more intimate level through fantasy fulfillment. It can add a rich, rewarding element to not only your relationship, but also a wonderful, enchanting spark to your sex life as well.

Embrace The Flame

Passionate kisses
filled with hot, burning desire,
stroking the flames into a raging inferno.

Under the midnight skies canopy
of a thousand stars watching
over our love making.

We struggle in the flame's embrace—
caught up in the spell of hot bodies,
hungry for the feel of searing skin.

Roving hands fumble at buttons
and zippers of too tight jeans,
pushed away in eager haste
to make way for the descent
into heaven.

CHAPTER NINE

▼

"SEX, LOVE AND ROCK AND ROLL"

We are assuming of course, in the writing of this book, that most of those who are reading this have had sex. What is sex? What about sex is so appealing? For one thing, it is one of the main motivational driving forces for all human beings.

Advertisements on television, radio, in magazines all sell using sex. Why? Because human beings, homo sapiens, are obsessed by the idea of sex, the beauty of sex and the actual act of sex itself.

Intercourse is another term that is generically used for sex. Making love. Most of us have learned in the process of sex, just how incredible it may feel. Now, we are also assuming that not all of you have had orgasms. But, they are inherent with sex. The thing we all strive for, at least some of the time, is the orgasm. The peak. However, in the actual act of sex, it does not necessarily have anything to do with love or with making love. You should make love 24 hours a day, 7 days a week in all you do and all you say.

Let's take sex to another level. Sex is about pleasure and passion. It is an absolute animal act of passion. Incredible, where lust takes over and love gets set aside. Any man will tell you that one. And women as well, when truly honest, will admit that they too love wild passionate, animal sex. That needs to be very, very explicitly understood, that sex and love do not necessarily go hand in hand. They don't necessarily even connect. They in fact, may have very little to do with each other. The actual act of sex is a very animalistic instinct. It is very passionate. And it is a release of passion from within us. When we are in the middle of those sexual passions, it would not make any difference who was doing it to you, with you or for you. For that particular instant, if you had a blindfold on, it just would not matter. Just as long as the pleasure did not stop. If they kept going and you reached that climax you were searching for, striving for, craving, more than anything else in the world at that given second, then it would not make much difference at that moment who you were with.

Now to say sex isn't better with somebody you love, would be lying. Because it is better, but why is it better? Let's examine that. We believe the reason it's better is because you know that person so well and you can trust them and again, we get back to the honesty, the trust and the acceptance and all the other things we have discussed. When all of those things are in place, then you can say things, do things, act out things, explore fantasies, move in ways that you would never do with a partner you did not know, a stranger.

The honest truth is that in the act of sex, you are at your most vulnerable. There is no time in your life when you are more revealing of who you are deep down inside than when you are in the act of passionate sexual intercourse.

I can not count the women, (I will count them by the dozens, dozens and dozens) who in the actual act of sex, can actually be "forced" to submit as a slave, actually call me master in the process. Afterwards, total denial. "I can't condone that type of thinking or anything else." However, in the actual throes of passion, they can and do say anything, do anything, to keep the sensations and feelings going. Sex is a very powerful medium. It's very seductive.

Often, women think when they have sex with a man they are in love with him. Men believe when they have sex they are in love with the woman. For that one moment in time, perhaps they are in love with the partner. They don't understand that what they are in love with is the animal passions that came out at that particular time. They haven't bothered to do the work in the relationship to learn the other aspects so it would be even better, even richer and truly loving.

Should you subjugate your animal passions? Well, in a relationship where you don't feel absolutely safe, that's what you do. It's hard to let go. I can think of experiences of my own, where the person that I was with professed and vowed to love me with all of their heart, but their actions didn't speak of that kind of love and therefore, I could not let go and cross that ultimate boundary, which was to reach complete physical satisfaction and to find that ecstasy I was looking for with that person. I didn't trust them with being that vulnerable and that open to let them see how wonderful this physical, animal act really is. I didn't trust them enough to let my "animal" loose. You have to build on all of the things that we are talking about with the trust and the acceptance, the honesty, the respect, the tolerance, everything, in order to have a complete sexual experience with your mate. You have to trust that person explicitly and they have to trust you explicitly. Otherwise it's just mechanics. Yes, for the man, mechanics might get him off, and for some women, mechanics will get her off, but you will never have the complete fulfillment of absolute openness and the writhing passion that is possible when you completely trust the person that you are with. You will never reach that place where the feeling is so joyous you can and do literally cry with joy.

You've been honest with your mate about what you want and what you desire. Now, you have to be willing to be completely open and honest about your fantasies and your sexual desires in order to be able to release everything that's inside of you, to unlock all the doors. All those places where you need to be scratched, so to speak. You can't let that go if you don't trust the person that you are with and if you haven't built some kind of a relationship.

Otherwise, what you are having is incredible sex. Nothing wrong with incredible sex, but it's not going to be emotionally fulfilling, spiritually fulfilling. Yes, it will be physically fulfilling and you might reach orgasm, but you won't have all of it without having built the bridges that we've talked about.

From the males point of view, we will say this. It's impossible for you as a male, to let all the animal instincts that are buried within you from millions of years of breeding out to the surface. You can not let them out if the female is not the type that you are completely capable of being honest with, that accepts you totally. If she doesn't respond to you in that manner, you are not going to open up. You are not going to let all that passion inside of you come up from the bottom. If she is, then you will take control of her completely in the bedroom.

Within each and every male lurks this passion. It's buried within us. It's given to us at birth and then it's suppressed, year after year, as we are raised, till by the time we are grown, there is little or anything left of the male there. Just the shell, the look of one, and I don't care if you work out and look like Mr. Universe or you wear horn rim glasses and sit behind a computer console. Within every single male lurks this ability and it can all come out if you are truthful, honest and accepting. And she is truthful, honest and accepting. Because she also has those passions, she loves being a slave to a master, a man that is the master in the bedroom, the master of his destiny, and can come in contact with the genetic heritage that was given to him at birth. Don't be afraid of it. Don't run from it. Embrace it, both of you. Embrace the femininity that's within you as a female. You were born on this planet with incredible attributes to be pleasing. Use them. And you as a male, you were born on this planet to please, to give pleasure. Give it. Don't be afraid of it. Don't be shy of it. Don't shirk your responsibility as a male. And don't shirk your responsibility as a female.

But what you also have to understand is that it's not a competition. It's never about competition between the two of you. It is about genuinely loving, trusting, caring for and desiring for your mate to have the ultimate pleasurable sexual experience.

Try new things. The worst thing that can happen in a relationship in regard to sex is to get stale. Obtaining sexual pleasure becomes a rut when the partners do not feel free to explore and fantasize and act upon those fantasies.

Try a little role playing from time to time. For example, you might pretend to be master and slave (and it doesn't matter who plays what role—you decide). One is the absolute obedient servant of the other and must do as "commanded." Or get a couple of masks and wear them during foreplay and even during intercourse itself for a whole new twist on the event.

And sex can be an event. It can be treated as an event. Make time for sex. Schedule it if necessary. Plan what you will do, what roles you will play. Have some fun! If nothing else, sex should be fun, for both partners. But it's not always about planning. Sometimes impromptu is better.

Don't be afraid to explore sex and experiment with sex. Sex is for the pleasure of each other. Your body is for the pleasure of your mate. Share your body in all its fullness and wholeness with your lover. Don't be ashamed of the most beautiful act in creation. Sex can and will deepen your love for and commitment to one another if you are willing to explore all of its myriad possibilities, including quickies.

Today, there are no real excuses for not enjoying your sex life fully and completely. If you are a man and you have difficulty at times or even frequently, with erections, there are drugs (we won't name names) that can help. The ability to get and maintain an erection does not have to be a problem. Yes, it may be embarrassing when it happens.

But in a loving relationship, that embarrassment can be talked about openly and honestly and you can both agree to try different things to make sex better for both of you. As medical science has proven, not being able to get or sustain an erection is in many, many cases, a physical problem, not an emotional or mental one. The blood vessels don't open up and allow the blood to flow into the penis as it did when you were 20 or 30. That is nothing to be ashamed of. Medical science has an answer if you are willing to accept there is a possible physical problem and research ways to handle it, rather than attempt to hide from the problem. In fact, we believe it does not need to be considered a "problem." It is simply one more thing to "design around."

If you can't take drugs for this issue, then open your mind and look at every possibility for achieving sexual pleasure with your mate. Men, if you can't get and maintain an erection for long enough to please your woman, then don't be afraid to try "toys" to help her achieve orgasm. The point is to please the other and in so doing, achieve pleasure yourself.

And women, don't be so selfish as to think that if he can't get the kind of erection he did when he was younger, that there is something wrong with you, and that you can't have pleasure. If you are willing to be open and explore other possibilities, you can still have an incredibly fulfilling sex life and both of you can achieve great pleasure from each other and with each other.

Men are visual creatures often when it comes to sex. We've heard it said that men think about sex over 200 times a day! That means about every 5 minutes or so, they're thinking in some form or other about sex. Women, you can use that to your advantage to achieve spectacular sex with your mate. Play to his visual imagery needs. Dress up. Be sexy. Be whatever it takes to please your man. We guarantee he will respond doubly in kind to make sure you are pleased as well.

And for those women who have physical problems also, there are remedies available as well. There are a multitude of lubricants to solve the potential drying problem. There are ways to solve any and every problem when it comes to a fulfilling sex life, if you are but willing to discuss, explore and try new ideas. Don't get stuck in a rut. Look for answers.

Have sex anywhere and everywhere and any time you feel like it. No, not on downtown main street, but anywhere (physically) that it's reasonable to do so and won't involve the long arm of the law interfering with your pleasure. Try a quickie in the airport parking garage when he comes back from a business trip. Try driving down back country roads and pulling into a heavily wooded area and having a quick romp. Yes, you may have to try unusual positions to accomplish this, but where there's a will, there's a way. Sneak off when you're at a party and indulge in a little hot foreplay in a spare bedroom, a closet or the bathroom. After all, no one will think it strange that a "couple" go off for a few minutes privately. And if they do, does it really matter? Don't let pride interfere with your excellent sexual pleasure. But do try to stay within the bounds of the law.

Spread a blanket in a secluded corner of a park and engage in some heavy necking. No one says sex is always about penetration. It is just as much about pleasurable feelings, regardless of how they are achieved.

Women, go with your man to a topless bar if that is something he likes doing. But open your mind and your heart and realize you are there for both of your pleasure. Don't let jealousy enter the picture. Enjoy the sights and sounds. Enjoy the eroticism of the dancers. If you are really brave, buy a dance for your man from the most beautiful woman in the place and then give him permission to enjoy himself. Let him know this "gift of pleasure" is from you because you love him.

Try surprising your mate. Fix a picnic lunch and take off for a secluded spot and indulge yourselves a bit.

Sex was meant to be joyous, not tedious. Sex was meant to be a glue that holds together a good relationship. It will never substitute, however, to hold together a poor relationship. Great sex will enhance and make stronger, a relationship that is built on the principals of trust, truth, honesty, compassion, acceptance, tolerance, forgiveness, respect and admiration. Practice all these things, and great sex will come naturally, the way it was meant to come.

Have we told you something here that you have never heard before? Probably not. Perhaps, however, we have put a new light, a new perspective on relationships and how to have a successful one. Is it hard work? You bet it is. Is it worth the effort? Absolutely!

EPILOGUE

▼

Trust is the main girder for your bridge to building a completely fulfilling, satisfying sexual relationship with your lover. Start small and build with time. You don't have to erect the Golden Gate Bridge the first time out. Just a small wooden bridge over a little creek will do for starters.

Honesty is the next support beam. First you must be honest with yourself about yourself. Search your soul and your heart. "Know thyself." Then you can move on to honesty about what you want in a relationship. And remember, lying by omission is still lying and deceitful and is as damaging to the bridge as would be the use of rusty materials or rotted lumber.

When your partner is truthful and honest with you, it is your responsibility to be accepting of him/her. We all want to be accepted for who we are. We can't change our mate. But we can change ourselves. We can design around problems and build bridges over the most vast of canyons if we desire to do so. We can throw the boomerang out filled with love, compassion, honesty, truth, acceptance and it will come back with those in kind.

Make the decision to accept your partner and stick with it. Don't let pride or misguided ideas disrupt your bridge building. Throw out the bricks that form walls. Give your partner the gift of respect and deferential regard. Put your partner above all others. Let your lover know how much you admire them and do it out loud. Allow your partner their feelings, beliefs, thoughts and don't prohibit them or oppose them. But be willing to also share your own, realizing that your partner may also have to tolerate something about you as well.

Get rid of the dynamite that is "bad" jealousy before it destroys the bridge you have so diligently been constructing. Look for positive ways to encounter and deal with "invasion of territory" by someone else. Guard the relationship through admiration, honesty, respect, truthfulness and tolerance.

Blow up the war museum. You are not keeping score or getting even. You are building a bridge to better communication, a healthier love for each other and extreme sex. When hurts occur, deal with them as calmly and rationally as possible without using the "you always" or "you never" type of statements. Those kind of statements are like setting a torch to that beautiful covered bridge you just completed. Even if it isn't burned to the ground, it will be severely damaged, perhaps beyond rebuilding.

Bridges can only be built if both parties agree to its design and style. You can't start on opposite sides with opposite ideas and expect to meet anywhere near the middle. Search for areas of compatibility and play those up. Spend as much time together as possible, especially early in a relationship so that you can learn how to build something as beautiful as the Brooklyn Bridge or the causeway across Lake Pontchartrain.

Let your imagination take flight in the bedroom (or wherever you choose). Start with simple fantasies. Just as you didn't learn how to build the Golden Gate Bridge the first time out, realize that your fantasy life is a learning, growing experience. Look for ways to satisfy your mate's fantasies and under no circumstances, be judgmental. Realize that fantasies are "make believe" and no one wants to live in the fantasy world all the time.

Explore your sexuality just as you would explore differing designs for bridges. All bridges are beautiful. So too are all aspects of the sexual relationship between partners. Be creative. Be inventive. And be open minded. Treat sex as the wonderful, joyous experience it was meant to be.

So go forward with each other in truth, trust, honesty, compassion, forgiveness, respect and avoid pride and jealousy and negative emotions that harm and destroy. Build bridges not walls. Build together. And have phenomenal sex while you discover your own happily ever after.

AFTERWORD

▼

If the content and information in this book intrigued you and you would like to know more, then watch for the upcoming *Flights of Fantasy*, an in depth look at the place of fantasy in a relationship and an exploration of the top fantasies of both men and women and how to fulfill them. If you enjoyed the poetry in this book, look for *Heart Songs, A Poetic Journey of Truth* by Victoria Lynn Dawson

ABOUT THE AUTHORS

Gilbert and Vicki Dawson have spent most of their adult lives married. Both married for the first time at the age of 17. Vicki was divorced after three years, then remarried one year later and was in that relationship for 21 years before divorcing again. Gilbert also divorced his first wife after three years and remarried several years later, then after thirteen years, divorced again. He remained single for over five years until meeting Vicki. They have been married to each other for 7 years and in the course of those years, have formed the kind of bond that other people are constantly asking about, wanting to know how they developed such a powerful, loving, trusting relationship. In answering those questions, the idea for this book was formed. They have four children between them.

Over the past several years, Mrs. Dawson has won numerous awards for her poetry, including honors from the Corpus Christi Byliners Texas Wide Writer's Competition, the Golden Triangle Writer's Guild, plus other awards from the Romance Writers of America, the Virginia Romance Writers, the Monterey Bay Chapter of Romance Writers and the Valley of the Sun Romance Writers. Her poetry has been published on numerous occasions and has always been well received. She has won Editor's Choice Awards for *The Book, Heart Threads, The Night Before-The Morning After, Empty Pockets.* These and more than 150 others are available in her collection, *Heart Songs, A Poetic Journey of Truth.*"